THE ILLUSTRATED GUIDE TO
VIKING
MARTIAL
ARTS

THE ILLUSTRATED GUIDE TO
VIKING
MARTIAL
ARTS

ANTONY CUMMINS

The
History
Press

Viking battle axes and spears found in the River Thames. (Courtesy Museum of London)

First published 2012

The History Press
The Mill, Brimscombe Port
Stroud, Gloucestershire, GL5 2QG
www.thehistorypress.co.uk

British Library Cataloguing in Publication Data.
A catalogue record for this book is available from the British Library.

ISBN 978 0 7524 8060 2

Typesetting and origination by The History Press
Printed in India.

CONTENTS

ACKNOWLEDGEMENTS

A special thank you to Todd Palmer for his essay on the Viking quotations that has allowed me to produce this work. *Viking Fighting Notes from 23 Sagas* was the foundation and inspiration for this book. Also to Jayson Kane for his work on the graphics, his noir style bringing the images to life.

About the Author

Antony Cummins is an author and historical researcher. Having obtained his Masters degree at the University of Manchester in Archaeology, he has worked as a TV presenter, documentary fact checker and writer. He is also the head of the Historical Ninjutsu Research Team who translate and publish medieval *ninja* training manuals from various clans of antiquity. As a martial artist, Antony has spent most of his martial arts life studying human movement and the dynamics of combat, concentrating on the Japanese arts but with the aim of understanding the universal principles of movement that define historical combat. For more information on his work visit his website: www.natori.co.uk

About the Graphic Designer

Jay Kane studied Art and Design in England and works as a freelance graphic designer. He has has worked alongside Antony Cummins for many years, realising his visions. Jayson lives in Stockport, England. For more information on his work, visit his website: www.iamjaykane.co.uk

THE SAGAS

The sagas referred to in this book were sourced from the Online Medieval and Classical Library (OMACL) and are a collection of public domain texts that are available to all. For further information, please view the full manuscripts on the OMACL website or the published sagas themselves. Each saga has been given a Roman numeral for ease of reference.

1

THE DEFINITION OF A 'VIKING'

The pounding of the surf, the call of a horn and the sight of a square sail on the horizon; you may be thinking that the next sound would be the troubled cry of a beachcomber screaming the word – Vikings! This may not have been the case. While the Anglo-Saxon word *Wicing* existed, we do not know when this word became the common name for all Scandinavian raiders, they may also have be called the *Danes, North-men* or other names. 'Viking' may be derived from the Old Norse word *vik*, meaning a bay, implying a Viking was one who kept his ship in a bay, or the Old English *wic*, meaning a camp or a trading place. However, the word Viking is used today to describe Scandinavian 'warrior-farmers' and/or Scandinavian privateers and raiders. It is not the intention of this book to list and identify the social differences in the Viking world, or to differentiate between those who were warrior-farmers and those who were professional sea raiders and privateers. The purpose is to attempt to reconstruct the fighting arts of all the people within the medieval Scandinavian world. No matter what they were called or how they were portrayed, we know that what we are dealing with is a group of men who are 'warrior-farmers' and that for the purposes of this book it does not matter if they were fighting in Scandinavia over land disputes, raiding monasteries or protecting the Dane-law in England. For this investigation into the martial arts of the Vikings, we have only to know that a 'Viking', as we have come to know them, was a Scandinavian who was part of a warrior culture with its own methods of fighting. Therefore, this book will refer to all Scandinavian warriors as 'Vikings', as that is the name by which they are now most commonly known.

✧ ANALYSING THE TEXTS

The first thing an academic would do is list the pitfalls in attempting to reconstruct the Viking martial arts by using the post-Viking era writings. These include:

1 The time delay between the events of the saga era and the recording of the sagas can average around 200 years.
2 The authors were writing for a specific audience.
3 The clothes, weapons and items of the world in the sagas actually reflect the Christian medieval period at the time of writing.
4 The subtleties of translation could lead to mistakes.
5 The writers embellished the feats of those in the stories beyond the reality.

These problems are all good reasons not to trust the word of the sagas. Most academics would say it is too problematic to get a correct martial understanding from them. However, the aim of this book is simply to take the basic elements of the combat as described and start to reconstruct them as a martial art, not to analyse the historical record in full. So this book becomes a starting point for all Viking enthusiasts to work from, as a guideline for reference. While some feel that the reality is too far away to grasp, the author feels that the truths that will be unearthed through this approach are worth the effort of tackling the problems that the saga writers have left for us.

Now that these problems are established we can identify the solutions. It is the job of the reader to consider these problems at all times and to take them into account when striving for the truth. With this in mind we now turn to the counter-arguments.

1 This issue is a great factor in reliability and we can imagine that many changes have been made, especially with the Christianisation of the country. However, if a man is decapitated in a story it is unlikely that this will change into a leg amputation or a spear thrust, such evolution would not be natural. We can trust that if in the written saga a man was defeated by having his leg removed, then we can expect that the original story held the same information. Remember that the audience was still a warrior culture, even if that of Christian knights, they were still descendants of the people in these sagas and 200 years is not a long time for an aristocracy to transform itself, nor is it such a long time that the stories could have radically changed, so that the combat descriptions became distorted wholesale, even if they had become somewhat embellished.

2 The sagas certainly were aimed at a certain audience. We have to consider the difference in the warrior aristocracy of the Viking era and the warrior aristocracy of the early Christian medieval period. Underneath the religious change you still have a selection of aristocratic families who fight with similar weapons for similar reasons of greed, land and pride. They simply want to hear stories of the brave and the heroic, which has no bearing on the martial arts issue.

3 The look of a Viking and the look of a Christian knight may seem radically different from an external point of view. However, if we take into account the only factors that would affect the martial arts, then we can see that the differences are slight: a sword in the twelfth and thirteenth century is very like its Viking equivalent. It is still well constructed, of similar length and weight. The spear is still a principal weapon, as is the axe, the warrior wears mail and a helm, as did the Vikings. The only changes to this fundamental equipment are in the shape of the shield, from what was probably a circular version to a kite shape, and the addition of small sections of plate mail being worn. The issue of the shield is germane and is discussed in the text. And there appears to be no mention of plate mail in the sagas.

4 This is the biggest issue and the most problematic. All the sagas here are late nineteenth-century or early twentieth-century academic translations. We know from the introduction to the new translations of The Sagas of the Icelanders that these older translations are more 'word for word' than later works. These older texts are therefore better for our purposes as they stay as close to the original as possible. It does not matter in general how the translator has come up with sentences such as 'his head was cleave in twain' or 'his leg was cut off below the knee', any translation is unlikely to be factually incorrect. Here we are not concerned with the subtle meanings or literary

skill of the work, we have used a small number of quotations that have direct meaning and are unlikely to be in error. This being said, it is still possible that translation may be the cause of some inaccuracies. On the whole, we have ignored ambiguous text references and poetic flourishes. We can use the most unambiguous quotations to begin to establish if groups of attack and defence methods can be categorised, and from these categorisations we can start to build the martial arts of the Vikings.

5   We have to remember that the audience for the sagas was a section of fighting men or people who have witnessed violence of a similar kind. So while there was embellishment, it was not in the realms of fantasy. Unrealistic embellishment about the Viking fighting arts at the time of writing would be like telling a story today in which a soldier of World War II shot and killed 500 men in an hour. The audience would simply refuse to believe it. The inclusion of demons, monsters and spirits has to be taken as a part of the world that they lived in, and heroic deeds were meant to be just outside of the reach of a warrior and relatively close to the reality of combat. Most of the descriptions are brutal and simple.

2

MARTIAL ARTS

As a martial artist and having spent a significant amount of time in Japan trying to find the 'secrets' behind the way of the warrior, I have learned a few lessons. Firstly, when martial artists from any style reach a certain level, they tend to gravitate towards the same form of movement from whatever school they come, that is – balanced, economical and potentially deadly. Secondly, most people concentrate on the differences between styles, whereas the similarities outweigh dissimilarities. As a historian, I find that the modern martial arts audience do not think in the way in which ancient warriors thought. It is not often that you find the likes of Julius Caesar writing that the Gauls are soft and weak, nor do Irish monks say that the fighting style of the Vikings is rudimentary and lacking in organisation or finesse. The Mongols and the Japanese did not consider each other as poor fighters. It is rare in history to find a chronicler opining that the warriors over the next mountain are weaklings and that their martial prowess is questionable. In general, all martial arts styles across the globe share a great deal in common – and any man trained in those arts from a young age is a man to be feared. We should not fall in to the trap of underestimating how far a fighter can push himself and the skill level that can be achieved in any art, especially one that results in death.

A deep understanding of the martial arts is a lifelong pursuit. However, for those who have had no formal training, here are some precepts that I feel to be universal:

- Movement should always start at the hips
- The body should move as one
- Power does not come from the arm or muscles alone
- Balance should be retained and small steps should be taken at all times
- You should never overreach but instead move in and strike
- Martial arts are not static and a fighter should move like a 'castle on wheels', opening his portcullis only to attack
- Movements must be dynamic, three dimensional and fluid

I have spent my life looking for the connections between all martial arts and the universal truths I have come to are that a well trained man moves with absolute efficiency and strikes with formidable power, be it kung-fu, jujutsu or fencing; and to be on the receiving end of a determined attack by a master normally results in death.

✧ THE WEAPONS AND THE IMAGES

Martial instruction books have consistently been plagued with drab pictures, grainy black and white photographs against a school hall gym background. The aim of this book is to merge three elements: historical research, martial arts instruction and noir style art, in a collaboration which should bring historical accuracy, art and entertainment together. That being said, it must be remembered that these images are graphical representations and therefore have limitations. Take note that at times, shields shown flat against the 'wall' of the image in reality would be covering any openings. The reader must take these images as two-dimensional representations of three-dimensional movement. The weapons in the images are artistic representations of the time period and may not match the saga descriptions completely. Taking both of the above points into consideration, Jayson Kane has done a wonderful job of creating a dynamic and inspirational martial arts guide.

Now that the stage is set and the problems identified, you have grasped the idea of martial arts and understand the approach taken to the weapons and to the style of the imagery, the opportunity to take an entirely new look at the world of the Viking warrior can be taken.

3

THE SWORD

'The sword ye have, Bersi, is longer than lawful'

The sword, from no matter what era or in any form, is the emblem of the highest forms of the martial arts. To hold a sword brings out the warrior in most men and to watch it swing in silver arcs through the air rouses the blood. The Viking sword is no different. This chapter on swordsmanship reveals the dynamics of Viking sword combat and the bloody truth found at the end of a blade. The sword was an expensive piece of equipment, often handed down from generation to generation. Early blades were made of strips of wrought iron twisted with mild steel that were then forged and a hardened edge (usually edges) added.

When thinking of swordsmanship do not think of the slow movements of 'sword and sandals' or 'merrie England' cinema, instead one should think of a very dynamic interaction between the combatants that usually only lasts for a short time before either a bloody end is brought about or the situation changes. The art of the sword in Viking times was fast and terminal.

✧ THE OVERHEAD CUT

This is a basic cutting action that can be found in all martial arts across the world. The primary target is the head with the intent of splitting the opponent's skull and it is a lethal cut in all its applications. It can be assumed that this cut was primarily done with a single handed grip and would probably have been delivered with a directional step to improve the power of the cut through body dynamics. It appears that this cut was not intended to be a lacerating cut but one that would cleave the head and the body using as much force as the attacker could muster while retaining balance. Such a cut is drastic and deadly, as can be seen by the references in the sagas. What is unknown is how this strike was initiated. In the *Katori Shinto-ryu* sword school of Japan this cut is started with the swordsman moving his hand upwards and to the left side of his head before he reaches the start of the downward cut. This is done to avoid the samurai's helmet and crest. A start similar to this is in Viking warfare is possible but not definite, as Viking helms did not have large crests or any obstructive decoration. However, if this cut is made while holding a shield then it would have to start in one of two ways. It would either have to swing around the front of the shield, as in the case with the samurai helmet, or it would have to come up to a position from the rear/right quarter. The downward swing of the sword could come from a wider possibility of angles if done without a shield.

Version 1: The Overhead Cut from around the shield.

Version 2: The Overhead Cut from the right quarter.

Saga References

Unsurprisingly, the references in the sagas show just how devastating a blow like this can be, either fatal or causing extreme maiming. Modern tests of replica weapons confirm how destructive a blow this is to the human body.

II

'Bardi, who was the swiftest of those men, and hewed at him with the sword Thorgaut's-loom, and hewed off well-nigh all the face of him'

'Now Thorgisl (Hermundson) smites a stroke on him down his nose from the brow, and said: "Now hast thou gotten a good mark befitting thee; and even such should more of you have." Then spake Thorgisl the Hewer: "Nought good is the mark; yet most like it is, that I shall have the heart to bear it manfully; little have ye yet to brag over." And he smote at him so that he fell and is now unfightworthy'

III

'axes hard driven, shields cleft and byrnies torn, helmets were shivered, skulls split atwain, and many a man felled to the cold earth'

III

'…and clave him down, both helm and head, and mail-clad body'

IV

'…and smote his sword into his head, and clave it down to the jaw-teeth'

V

'Then An went into the dairy hard and swift, and held his shield over his head, turning forward the narrower part of it. Bolli dealt him a blow with Footbiter, and cut off the tail-end of the shield, and clove An through the head down to the shoulder, and forthwith he gat his death.' [Here we see evidence of anachronism. The author is describing a kite shield and not the earlier round version attributed to the saga age.]

VI

'Dromund took the sword, at once raised it aloft and struck a blow at [a shallow] angle. It came into his head with such force that it penetrated to his jaw'

'As Vigbjod bent down to pull his sword clear again, Onund dealt him a blow on his shoulder, severing his arm and disabling him'

'First he went for Steinolf of Hraundal and cleft his skull down to his shoulders'

XI

'Now the king takes his sword Kvernbit with both hands, and hewed Eyvind through helm and head, and clove him down to the shoulders'

✧ THE STRIKE TO THE NECK

This is a strike with the sword to an area of the neck with the intention of decapitation. The angle of attack may vary and will depend upon the situation that the swordsman is in and his relative position to his enemy. However, we can establish that version 1 is a cut made to an opponent's face and directed to the left side of his neck above the shield line. We see this strike in all swordplay. The Japanese have a similar cut called *Kesa-Giri*, which is usually executed with a forward step. This cut is meant to cut across the top of the collar bone and to the opposite armpit.

There is a third cut, which is not illustrated here. The sagas reference decapitation from behind or simply a straightforward decapitation with the opponent stood in an erect position. This would constitute a third version, however the cut is identical to the 'Horizontal Cut' (version 2) described further on in this chapter and is simply a neck level version of this strike.

Version 1: A strike to the side of the neck.

Version 2: It is also probable that this cut was made on the opposite side and that the swordsman moved his sword to his left and struck at the right side of the opponent.

Saga References

Decapitation is a prime method of killing in a warrior culture; the concept of the 'head cult' or 'head-hunting' is found throughout most warrior cultures and is clearly evident in the Viking world. What is interesting to note is that sometimes it may come as a surprise attack and be done from behind as an assassination, as opposed to a duel.

II

'Thorbiorn leaps at Bardi, and smites him on the neck, and wondrous great was the clatter of the stroke, and it fell on that stone of the beads which had been shifted [as when] he took the knife and gave it to Nial's son; and the stone brake asunder, and blood was drawn on either side of the band, but the sword did not bite'

III

'Let him smite the head from off him then, and be only lord of all that gold'

'…and therewith he drew his sword Gram and struck off Regin's head'

VII

'Then Flosi came up and hewed at Helgi's neck, and took off his head at a stroke'

'So he ran in up the hall, and smote Gunnar Lambi's son on the neck with such a sharp blow, that his head spun off on to the board before the king and the earls, and the board was all one gore of blood, and the earl's clothing too'

XIV

'Then Kalf struck at him on the left side of the neck'

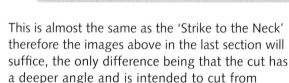 ## THE DOWNWARD STRIKE TO THE SHOULDER

This is almost the same as the 'Strike to the Neck' therefore the images above in the last section will suffice, the only difference being that the cut has a deeper angle and is intended to cut from the shoulder joint down to the opposite hip, thus using the images from the last technique there can be the following two versions.

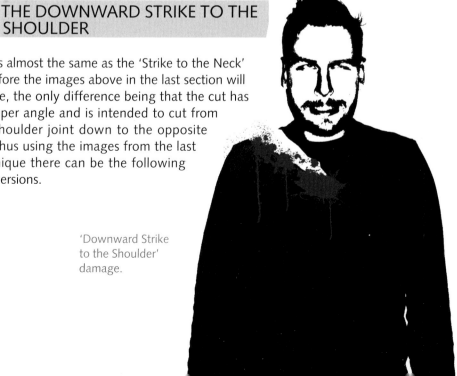

'Downward Strike to the Shoulder' damage.

Version 1

The cut is intended to cut the human torso in half from a diagonal angle and could be said to exactly replicate the Japanese *Kesa-Giri* cut mentioned above.

Version 2

As with the 'Strike to the Neck' cut, it is possible to make this cut from the opposite side, especially if the swordsman does not have a shield in hand. If the swordsman is using a shield then he would have to either dip the shield and turn the edge towards his neck so that it did not obstruct the blade or he would have to expose the inside of his shield and open his body to attack. This would only be done if the strike was a powerful full step and a fully committed stroke. Alternatively, it could involve an extension of the arm and a strong 'flick' style execution, an attempt to sever the shoulder muscles and disable the arm. However, this last cut is merely speculation as most of the references talk of a 'mighty blow' and severed limbs, which probably came from the swordsman's right and dominant side.

Saga References

This appears to be a most devastating and powerful blow and usually ends a fight and is effective even if the sword does not 'bite'. A crushed collar bone or severed arm both result in the loss of use of the limb. One must remember that the opponent would have to be without shield or the swordsman would have to have used a gap in a shield-bearer's defence to make this cut.

I

'She blunted Cormac's sword, so that it would not bite, but yet he struck so great a stroke on Thorvard's shoulder that the collarbone was broken and his hand was good for nothing'

The Upper Shield Cleave. The attacker here is striking into the shield of the defender to use it to pull him off balance.

II

'Now Eyolf smiteth at Odd, and it came on to his cheek and on to his mouth, and a great wound was that' [the angle from the cheek to mouth would indicate this cut but just to the face]

V

'Bolli hewed in return, and struck Lambi's shoulder, and the sword flew down along the side of him, and he was rendered forthwith unfit to fight'

'Thorgils was standing near, and struck after him with a sword, and caught him on the shoulder and made a great wound'

VI

'Then he quickly seized the short sword which he was wearing, drew it and struck at the troll's right shoulder, cutting off her right arm and releasing himself'

VII

'Then Kari smites at him, and the sword fell on his shoulder, and the stroke was so mighty that he cleft in twain shoulder, arm, and all, and Snowcolf got his death there and then'

'…but Gudleif smote him on the shoulder and hewed his arm off, and that was his death'

✧ THE UPPER SHIELD CLEAVE

This is the exact same cut as the 'Downward Strike to the Shoulder' in its execution. The difference is that the cut is intended for the shield and not for the person or that the shield is used to block the 'Downward Strike to the Shoulder'. Thus, it is not the technique that makes this cut different but its application. We know from the sagas and modern experimentation that a shield could be cleaved and it is only then a short step to conclude that to do so was part of the Viking sword arts, to be used to render a shield unusable for the duration of the fight and thus opening up the defences of the opponent. This theory is supported by the fact that there is the counter-move of the 'Sword Disarm', explained in the shield use chapter.

Saga References

This seems to be a regular occurrence in the sagas and it seems quite reasonable for a swordsman to expect his shield to be shattered. The duelling system of 'three shields' reflects the knowledge that one's shield will be a target.

I

'Bersi struck the first blow, and cleft Cormac's shield'

'But Bersi leapt up, slashed at him, and clove his shield. The sword-point was at Steinar's breast when Thord rushed forth and dragged him away, out of reach'

The Lower Shield Cleave. The swordsman here has damaged the lower part of the opponents' shield.

VII

'Kol hews at him, and the blow fell on Thrain's shield, and cleft it down from top to bottom'

'He cut at once at Hrut's shield, and clove it all in two, from top to point'

✧ THE LOWER SHIELD CLEAVE

This is also a variation of the 'Downward Strike to the Shoulder' but is executed to the lower part of the opponent's body. Again it is questionable as to whether this is an attack against the shield itself or if it is an attack that is blocked by the opponent's shield. The key to this technique is that it shows that Viking swordsmanship incorporated a multiple level attacking concept. In the Japanese tradition this is dissected into three areas, *Jodan*, *Chudan* and *Gedan* – high, middle and low level, respectively. This simple point is of high importance as it shows a much more dynamic and three-dimensional spatial awareness during combat than we have come to expect from modern Viking representations.

Saga References

That a shield could be sliced in two is not difficult to believe having witnessed the Japanese cutting art of *Tameshigiri*; the issue that arises is the structure of the Viking shield. We believe that some shields had iron-rimmed edges and some did not. Therefore, is the cut that cleaves the shield in two delivered to a shield with an iron rim, or is the blow only successful against a shield without such a defensive rim – depending on the thickness of course? This would only be established by test cuts and for the time being will have to remain speculation.

I

'He struck the shield-edge, and the sword glanced off, slit Bersi's buttock, sliced his thigh down to the knee-joint, and stuck in the bone. And so Bersi fell'

VI

'The Viking dashed forward, reached Onund and hewed at him with his sword, which cut right through his shield and into the log beneath his leg, where it remained fixed'

VI

'Then he turned upon Gunnar himself and struck a blow that severed his shield right across below the handle, and the sword struck his leg below the knee. Then with another rapid blow he killed him'

VII

'But when Helgi heard that, he cast away the cloak. He had got his sword under his arm and hewed at a man, and the blow fell on his shield and cut off the point of it, and the man's leg as well.' [Again, this appears to be a kite-shaped shield of later origin than the saga era]

Version 1: Severing the Arms. The swordsman uses his shield to defend his own arm and attacks the outstretched forearm of the opponent.

Version 2: There are many variations on this cut, it is also possible to perform an upward strike with the back of the sword.

✧ SEVERING THE ARMS

This is a fundamental technique used in other Medieval European and also Japanese swordsmanship and appears to be a staple in the Viking fighting arts. Most modern swordsmen undervalue the effectiveness of attacking the extended forearms for the subconscious reason that a killing stroke is thought only to be delivered to the torso or head. The severing of an arm will undoubtedly halt the fight or bring it to a bloody end. The swordsman will still need to stay well guarded until the opponent falls through loss of blood or cannot react having succumbed to the pain or shock. An opponent can normally still deliver a strike that has started, even if he has received a death blow himself. Talhoffer, one of the most well-known swordsmen of the Medieval European tradition, illustrates this move in one of his *Fechbüch* or fight-books, as do other masters. The basic principle is to wait for an opponent's strike and for you to counter strike by aiming for his extended arm.

Saga References

The main issue with a cut to the arms is armour. In Japanese swordsmanship this cut can be executed in two ways. Without armour the sword is swung in an arc to cut off the hands, whereas when armoured, the sword is placed on the wrist and drawn across the target to lacerate the exposed area. Whether this distinction was made in Viking combat is only speculation and would be dependent on the type of arm protection, if any, that a Viking may have been wearing. (The last quotation does not involve swordplay, but it is irresistible.)

VI

'Grettir aimed a blow at him with his sword and cut off his paw just above the claws'

'Then Grettir sprang on to the crossbenches near the door. Gunnar's hands and the shield were still inside the door, and Grettir struck down between him and the shield, cutting off both his hands at the wrist. He fell backwards out of the door, and Grettir gave him his death-blow'

VII

'Gunnar cut at Hallgrim's arm hard, and lamed the forearm, but the sword would not bite'

'Then Skiolld cut off his hand, and he still kept them off with his other hand for some time'

'… but he brandished his sword so quickly that no eye could follow it, and he made a blow with the sword, and it fell on Hallbjorn's arm above the wrist, so that it cut it off'

'Gunnar smites off Otter's hand at the elbow-joint'

XIII

'There sat also a very handsome man with long hair, who twisted his hair over his head, put out his neck, and said, 'Don't make my hair bloody.' A man took the hair in his hands and held it fast. Thorkel hewed with his axe; but the Viking twitched his head so strongly that he who was holding his hair fell forwards, and the axe cut off both his hands'

✧ THE HORIZONTAL CUT

This is not a static and formulaic cut, it can be done at any height and from any position, be it two-handed or single-handed, with the blade horizontal, or tilted up or even down. The criteria is that the blade goes from left to right or right to left in some form of stroke that runs horizontally.

Saga References

It is a common belief that only a Japanese sword could cut a body in two, as it is often recorded. This common misconception that the Katana is more effective at cutting is a result of not understanding the origins of the Katana's fame. The qualities that a Katana holds over any other sword are its ability to retain a cutting edge and its flexibility; the sharpness is of no consequence. If any sword is sharp enough and can withstand the impact of the cut, then it will succeed in the same cut (assuming of course that the swordsman has the necessary technique and power). Documented sword tests show the ability of western swords to cut a human in two. What prevents complete division is the mail shirt. We know that a body can be cut in two, but as seen in the saga quotes, the sword often does not bite but results in crushed ribs, which is the likely outcome of an enemy wearing chain mail. There is sparse archaeological evidence for chain mail being worn by the Vikings, an expensive accoutrement; a single mail shirt was excavated in Scandinavia at Haugsbygd in Norway. Some have argued that the Vikings may have worn leather armour, being more flexible and lighter, but there is no physical evidence for this.

I

'The Viking laid bare his side, but the sword would not bite upon it'

'At last Cormac smote upon Thorvard's side so great a blow that his ribs gave way and were broken; he could fight no more'

II

'Bardi slashed into the side of him, and Ketil fell'

IV

'He was not wounded, because no weapon might bite on his kirtle' [this could represent any of the body strikes, however it is cited here as an example of torso strikes]

'Steinthor brought his sword down on Freystein above his hips, and smote the man asunder in the midst'

VI

'…then he struck at Thorgils the son of Ingjald and almost cut him in two'

'Then the giant tried to reach up backwards to a sword which was hanging in the cave, and at that moment Grettir struck at him and cut open his lower breast and stomach so that all his entrails fell out into the river and floated down the stream'

Version 1: The archetypal 'Horizontal Cut' is from the right side of the body to the left at waist height with the intention of opening the gut or to cut the opponent in half.

Version 2: The cut can also be aimed higher and at neck level and thus creates a true 'Cut to the Neck' which will give a clean decapitation or it can be delivered to the nose bridge of a helmet, which effectively blinds the opponent; or the same cut is aimed at the shoulders and breast.

'It passed across his shoulder, out under his right arm, and cut him right in two. His body fell in two parts on top of Grettir and prevented him from recovering his sword as quickly as he wished' [This cut fits best within this chapter as the opponent is twisted in mid-air.]

VII

'Gunnar sees this and was swift to smite at the Easterling, and cuts him asunder at the waist'

'Then Kari rushes at him, and hews at him on the breast with his sword, and the blow passed at once into his chest, and he got his death there and then'

'Kari made a sweep at that same man with his sword, and cut him asunder at the waist'

'Then Thorstein Geirleif's son rushed at Kari, and thought to take him in flank, but Kari caught sight of him, and swept at him with his sword across the shoulders'

XIII

'There Thorstein Midlang cut at Bue across his nose, so that the nosepiece of his helmet was cut in two, and he got a great wound'

XIV

'He struck the lenderman before mentioned [Thorgeir of Kviststad] across the face, cut off the nose-piece of his helmet, and clove his head down below the eyes so that they almost fell out'

'King Olaf hewed at Thorer Hund, and struck him across the shoulders; but the sword would not cut, and it was as if dust flew from his reindeer-skin coat'

✧ THE MID-LEVEL STRIKE TO THE LEG

This is a cut that replicates the 'Downward Strike to the Shoulder' but is executed at a much lower level and is aimed between the thigh and the knee joint. The purpose is to dismember at this point forcing the opponent to yield or die. As with all the cuts that replicate the 'Downward Strike to the Shoulder' it is possible to execute it on both the left and right sides of the body. This cut can also be done by the swordsman in a low crouch.

Saga References

When a leg is severed in the sagas, one of two things normally happens. Either the person stops fighting and falls down dead through loss of blood; or they survive and then bargain for their lives. In such a case it appears from the sagas that three marks of silver will secure quarter and is a 'legal' way out of a duel. It is also noteworthy that 'peg-legs' were crafted for those who lost a leg in combat.

I

'Then Ogmund whirled about his sword swiftly and shifted it from hand to hand, and hewed Asmund's leg from under him'

'The Mid-level Strike to the Leg'. The swordsman can raise his sword on either his left or right side and make the cut from a standing position allowing the hips to 'fall' during the attacking step to insert power into this cut.

V

'Thorleik struck him with his sword, and it caught him on the leg above the knee and cut off his leg, and he fell to earth dead'

VI

'...and Grettir hewed at his right thigh, cutting out all the muscles so that he could fight no more'

'Kolskegg turned sharp round, and strode towards him, and smote him with his short sword on the thigh, and cut off his leg'

VII

'Thrain hews at Kol, and the stroke came on his leg so that it cut it off'

'Skarphedinn smites at Hallgrim's thigh, so that he cut the leg clean off'

'Kari came up just then, and cut off Leidolf's leg at mid-thigh, and then Leidolf fell and died at once'

'Kari leant on one side and smote at Glum with his sword, and the blow fell on his thigh, and took off the limb high up in the thigh, and Glum died at once'

✧ THE LOW-LEVEL STRIKE TO THE LEG

This is a cut intended to sever the leg at any point from below the knee down to the ankle. This again is a sub-genre of the 'Downward Strike to the Shoulder', however, this time there is a fundamental difference in stance and posture and therefore it has been divided into two versions.

Saga References

This type of wound seems to appear much less in the saga references, which suggests this move was executed more rarely or its success was significantly less then the 'Mid-Level Strike to the Leg'. It would take a highly trained fighter with battle experience to have the subconscious reaction time to take advantage of such an opening.

IV

'Thorarin cut the leg from Thorir at the thickest of the calf, and slew both his fellows'

VII

'Grim cut off Skiolld's foot at the ankle-joint'

'There was a man who ran up to Kari's side, and meant to cut off his leg, but Bjorn cut off that man's arm'

Version 1: The cut can be achieved by leaning forward with the shoulders and extending the arm so that the blade reaches the lower leg. The problem with this cut is that it opens the fighting stance and exposes the arm allowing for an easy counter strike. See the third quotation: 'There was a man who ran up to Kari's side, and meant to cut off his leg, but Bjorn cut off that man's arm.' It is unsure which section of the leg that the man is aiming for; however, both upper and lower leg targets could be applicable here. That being said, the 'Low-Level Strike to the Leg' would leave the attacking arm more exposed.

Version 2: The second version would be for the swordsman to crouch or semi crouch as he made his strike. This would open up the top of his head for attack but is a possible version of this technique.

At cut of this magnitude would be devastating and kill an opponent. Sword cutting tests show a clean cut through bone but also that the cut can of course be stopped by the second leg.

✧ CUTTING THROUGH BOTH LEGS

This is a cut that severs both of the legs from under an opponent leaving him bleeding to death. We can assume that the cut was more than likely to have been executed at an angle, cutting through the first leg at a higher point as the sword angles down.

Saga References

There is no reason to doubt the effectiveness of this cut, we can see evidence of victims at the Battle of Wisby (or Visby) in 1361, where a number of people took cuts to the lower legs. The Battle of Wisby took place on the island of Gotland not too long after the sagas were written down. Many of those killed were buried with their armour, a treasure trove for archaeologists, possibly because the bodies began to decompose in the heat before they could be stripped.

VII

'Then Gunnar cut both his legs from under him'

'Kolskegg saw that and cut off at once both Augmund's legs from under him, and hurled him out into Rangriver, and he was drowned there and then'

'…but afterwards he hewed off both of Asbrand's feet from under him'

✧ THE THRUST AND STAB

This is not to be mistaken for a lunge. A thrust of this nature is a driven attack which was probably executed from a much closer distance than an extended lunge and was most likely aimed around the solar plexus, breast and beneath the ribcage area, with the intent of piercing a vital organ. This thrust was probably done in one of two ways.

Saga References

Generally, stabbing an opponent is in itself an attempt at a coup de grace, for a sword thrust through a body is a dead sword unless it can be taken out with speed. A real martial encounter – especially when it's a life or death situation – is a collection of subconscious reactions to external aggression, and conscious decisions are seldom ever made. It has to be considered if it is easy to withdraw a sword from a body or not, which would affect how much this strike was practised. The fact that swords were double-edged suggests that thrusts were not uncommon, that they were always an option.

III

'Gudrun took a sword and thrust it through the breast of King Atli'

'Now crept the worm down to his place of watering, and the earth shook all about him, and he snorted forth venom on all the way before him as he went; but Sigurd neither

Version 1: The 'One-handed Thrust' is where the swordsman is up close and personal and uses the sword in one hand to skewer the body of the opponent. This is more than likely a single attack, which either results in the death of the opponent if successful or results in the swordsman retreating to a defensive position if unsuccessful.

trembled nor was adread at the roaring of him. So whenas the worm crept over the pits, Sigurd thrust his sword under his left shoulder, so that it sank in up to the hilts; then up leapt Sigurd from the pit and drew the sword back again unto him, and therewith was his arm all bloody, up to the very shoulder'

V

'Then she drew a sword and thrust it at Thord and gave him great wounds, the sword striking his right arm and wounding him on both nipples. So hard did she follow up the stroke that the sword stuck in the bolster'

VI

'Grettir got his sword, ran it into the heart of the bear and killed him'

VII

'Then Thangbrand thrusts a sword into his breast, and Gudleif smote him on the arm and hewed it off'

'Then Kari thrust at Lambi with his sword just below the breast, so that the point came out between his shoulders, and that was his deathblow'

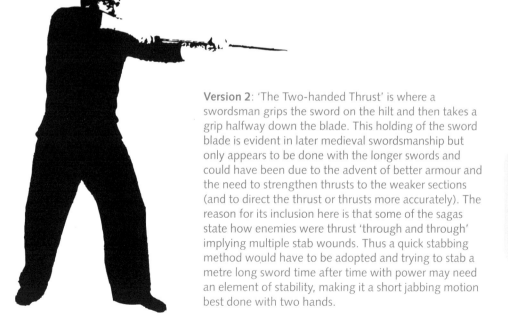

Version 2: 'The Two-handed Thrust' is where a swordsman grips the sword on the hilt and then takes a grip halfway down the blade. This holding of the sword blade is evident in later medieval swordsmanship but only appears to be done with the longer swords and could have been due to the advent of better armour and the need to strengthen thrusts to the weaker sections (and to direct the thrust or thrusts more accurately). The reason for its inclusion here is that some of the sagas state how enemies were thrust 'through and through' implying multiple stab wounds. Thus a quick stabbing method would have to be adopted and trying to stab a metre long sword time after time with power may need an element of stability, making it a short jabbing motion best done with two hands.

The swordsman taking two short running steps to pierce the neck, face or upper body of the opponent.

VIII

'Yngve had a short sword upon his knees, and the guests were so drunk that they did not observe the king coming in. King Alf went straight to the high seat, drew a sword from under his cloak, and pierced his brother Yngve through and through'

XII

'Now when they came to the house they attacked the king, and Herse Klyp, it is said, ran him through with his sword and killed him'

XVIII

'One of the heathens in particular fought so bravely, and ventured so near, that he came quite up to the castle-gate, and pierced the man who stood outside the gate with his sword'

✧ THE LEAP AND THRUST

This is possibly the closest we have to a classic lunge but this technique may have actually not been employed and may simply be a description of a fast attack with an aggressive step before an attack. One should not think of it as a classical lunge but as a charging thrust with one or two steps, or as a small 'leap' forward to put weight behind the blade.

Saga References

V

'…and when Bolli saw this he leapt forward at Helgi with Footbiter in his hand, and thrust Helgi through with it, and that was his deathblow'

VII

'Then Vebrand and Asbrand the sons of Thorbrand ran up to Kari, but Kari flew at Vebrand and thrust his sword through him'

Asleep in his bed, the opponent does not see the swordsman approach and deliver the fatal strike.

✧ THE DOWNWARD STAB

This is itself not a martial move but an assassination strike. Killing someone in their bed does occur a few times in the sagas. Though it may not represent martial combat, it does remind us of the realities behind the 'chivalric' world that we as a modern audience tend to see in medieval combat. We even think of the Viking as a 'noble savage' who would kill his enemies and duel with his own kind. However, we do find surprise assassinations throughout most of the sagas and the retribution that they bring.

Saga References

This type of action leads us into the world of the Viking age and shows us a glimpse of the true barbarity sometimes found there. In the Icelandic sagas there are accounts of people creeping into a main hall at night and being mistaken for one of the kinsman, while in reality, they are there to assassinate. If this type of assassination did take place, it is difficult to comprehend the self-control it would take, walking at night through a hall of warriors to kill and then walk back out and ride across moors and fens to get back to the safety of one's farm.

'But the third time he went in, and there lay Sigurd asleep; then Guttorm drew his sword and thrust Sigurd through in such wise that the sword point smote into the bed beneath him; then Sigurd awoke with that wound'

✧ THE TWO-HANDED CUT

This is the act of using both hands on the sword hilt to execute a cut with more power. The Viking weapon is normally one-handed, so where did they position their second hand for this stroke? It would be reasonable to conclude that the swordsman put his thumb and index finger between the hilt and the top lip of the pommel while wrapping the rest of the fingers around the pommel itself. The only other alternative is that it was held in the later medieval style, using the sword as a pole-arm, which does not fit well with the texts.

Saga References

I

'That shall not be,' cried Bersi; and took up his other sword, Whitting, two-handed, and smote Thorkel his deathblow

VI

'There was a hard struggle between them; Grettir used his short sword with both hands and they found it not easy to get at him'

✧ THROWING THE SWORD

This is the act of launching the sword at an assailant with the aim of either hitting the enemy with the pommel or piercing him with the blade. It is unknown if this was an established technique, a one-off, or simply fantasy. A small number of sword throwing

While basic in nature, the 'Two-handed Cut' would be a formidable blow that could be delivered with speed and could also come from any direction.

If this was ever a technique used in medieval combat, it would be an emergency move, a high stakes gamble, as it would result in the loss of the swordsman's primary weapon.

examples in history do exist. Renowned Japanese swordsman Miyamoto Musashi (c. 1584–1645) was reputedly able to throw his short sword with a high proficiency. The only practical advice that could be given here is that, to make this work, it would be better if the sword only rotates through half a circle, so it is thrown blade first, over a very short distance, in what is now called 'no spin'.

Saga References

What is uncertain in the next quotation is if the sword blade entered his back or if it was simply a bludgeoning hammer that knocked him to the floor. Did people possess the ability to throw a sword a short distance and have it stick like a spear, or did they throw the sword with the intent to strike and hold out for luck?

Version 1: This proposed method is done by holding the sword in a normal grip and delivering the blow in a 'hammer-hand' style to the opponents face or head – as can be seen in the fourth picture.

'Guttorm gat him unto the door; but therewith Sigurd caught up the sword Gram, and cast it after him, and it smote him on the back, and struck him asunder in the midst, so that the feet of him fell one way, and the head and hands back into the chamber'

✦ PUMMELLING

This is the act of hitting the opponent with the pommel of your sword and is the origin of the word pummelling. There is only one quote and it is ambiguous. However, it is not a far stretch of the imagination to consider that the Vikings would have used the heavy pommel to inflict damage.

Version 2: Western medieval combat has the technique called the 'Murder Stroke' and is found in most versions of western swordsmanship from the Middle Ages. Therefore, it is not impossible to consider that the Vikings had an antecedent to this move. The 'Murder Stroke' is done by reversing the sword and gripping it by the blade with the intent to use it as a war-hammer.

Saga References

People often question version 2, the 'Murder Stroke' and wonder about the damage such a move would do to your own hands. But a blade, to cut, has to make contact with skin, draw the skin to its extreme and then slice in a cutting motion. Therefore this cut would not seriously injure the hands. However, most people would surely attempt this with gloves or gauntlets on.

VI

'When he saw that the boy was within reach he raised his sword aloft and struck Arnor's head with the back of it such a blow that the skull broke and he died'

✧   SUNDERING A WEAPON

This is the act of cutting the wooden haft of any mounted blade with the intention of disarming the enemy. The act of cutting the haft of a weapon has countless variations and as such, it is impossible to list them here. The swordsman under attack must use the opponent's direction as a lead to make his cut against his opponent's weapon. There are two basic variations of this action:

- Stepping on the inside of his attack so that you are facing each other and then cutting at his weapon.
- Stepping on the outside of his attack to outflank him and then cutting at his weapon.

Saga References

Could a Viking sword cut through a wooden haft? The first reaction might be that, if a Viking sword can cut through a body and bones, then why not a wooden haft? Well, the modern replicas of weapons today are in general, poor imitations. A wooden haft of the Viking age may have been made of relatively thick hardwood, possibly leather-bound or even reinforced with iron and – even tougher – seasoned wood. So did this technique cut the haft?

VI

'Grettir struck back with his sword and cut through the shaft [of the spear]'

In this sequence, the swordsman is
on the inside of the opponent's strike.

Here, the swordsman is on the outside of the opponent's strike.

VII

'First, Glum Hildir's son rushed at them, and thrust at Kari with a spear; Kari turned short round on his heel, and Glum missed him, and the blow fell against the rock. Bjorn sees that and hewed at once the head off Glum's spear'

'After that they fall on him, and he breaks a spear of each of them, so well did he guard himself'

'Skarphedinn dashes the spearhaft in two'

'Hroald had a spear in his hand, and Hogni rushes at him; Hroald thrusts at him, but Hogni hewed asunder the spear-shaft with his bill, and drives the bill through him'

✧ THE PARRY AND CUT

This is moving the opponent's attack out of the way with an attack of your own against his incoming weapon and then following up with a counter strike. In many sword schools around the world the parry is a basic element of swordplay and these come in a myriad

forms, from the grace of the foil to the more weighty long sword parry. A parry can be achieved in a multitude of ways delivered from many angles, especially with a sword on sword. However, it can be broken down into four major areas. Parry the opponent's sword or spear to the left of the right, opening yourself for a cut on your return stroke or to parry upwards or downwards, or even to the quarters. The main point here is to simply avert the opponent's sword while retaining balance and stability over your centre of gravity, which allows you to counter with power and steadiness.

Saga References

The word parry suggests a graceful flick of the wrist. In this case however, you should consider the parry as a small but strong blow that knocks the opponent's sword or weapon off its trajectory.

A simple parry and return – the swordsman knocks the opponent's weapon to his right and counters with a thrust to the face; remember, countless variations can be based on this theme.

I

'Then Thorolf of Spakonufell set upon Cormac and struck at him. He warded off the blow'

IV

'…he ran at Thrand, and thrust at him with a spear, but Thrand put the thrust from him, and smote Raven on the arm close by the shoulder, and struck off the arm'

VII

'Then down fell the bill, and Gunnar seized the bill, and thrust Hallgrim through.'
[Technically, movement of the opponent's weapon off its line of attack.]

4

THE SPEAR

The spear is in the background of the Viking image, always there on the edge of our projection. In fact, the spear, along with all the pole-arms which are included here, can be classified as a Viking's primary weapon. The spear attacks clearly outnumber the sword attacks and seem to be more devastating at times. One advantage the sword appears to have over the spear is that a strike to the relatively unprotected lower legs with a sword will result in death or surrender, whereas a spear cut there does not normally end the combat. However, the spear is a very dynamic weapon, to thrust, to throw and cut with, it was an active reaching weapon, not used simply to tap and prod as we see at re-enactments and in films. From catching spears mid-flight, throwing impaled enemies from roofs and swiping at legs, spear combat in the Viking age appears to have been one of dynamic movement and flights of iron lightning bolts.

✧ THE SPEAR THROW

The spear was thrown with the intent of disarming a shield or impaling an opponent. The technique of spear throwing is universal and needs no description here.

Saga References

The third saga quotation here is similar to a Roman tactic where a *Pilum* was prepared for flight in a similar manner, with the intent that it could not be thrown back at its owner. The sheer number of references points to its extensive use.

III

'Many a spear and many an arrow might men see there raised aloft'

V

'Before they met, Kjartan flung his spear, and it struck through Thorolf's shield above the handle, so that therewith the shield was pressed against him, the spear piercing the shield and the arm above the elbow, where it sundered the main muscle, Thorolf dropping the shield, and his arm being of no avail to him through the day'

VI

'Grettir got off his horse. He had a helmet on his head, a short sword by his side, and a great spear in his hand without barbs and inlaid with silver at the socket. He sat down and knocked out the rivet which fastened the head in order to prevent Thorbjorn from returning the spear upon him … Neither of them had a helmet. Grettir went along the marsh and when he was within range launched his spear at Thorbjorn. The head was not so firm as he had intended it to be, so it got loose in its flight and fell off on to the ground'

VII

'Atli grasped the spear, and hurled it after him. Then Brynjolf cast himself down on the ground, but the spear flew away over him'

'A little while after Gunnar hurls the bill at Bork, and struck him in the middle, and the bill went through him and stuck in the ground'

'…and with that he snatched up a spear and hurled it at him, and hit him under the chin, and Aslak got his death wound there and then'

'Thangbrand shot a spear through Thorwald'

'Kari, and Grim, and Helgi, threw out many spears, and wounded many men; but Flosi and his men could do nothing'

'Flosi snatched the spear from him, and launched it at Ingialld, and it fell on his left side, and passed through the shield just below the handle, and clove it all asunder, but the spear passed on into his thigh just above the knee-pan, and so on into the saddle-tree, and there stood fast'

The launch of a spear would depend upon the distance it had to travel and the trajectory would have to be changed depending on the situation. The trajectory here implies relatively close combat.

'Then he launched the spear back over the river. Flosi sees that the spear is coming straight for his middle, and then he backs his horse out of the way, but the spear flew in front of Flosi's horse, and missed him, but it struck Thorstein's middle, and down he fell at once dead off his horse'

'men thought that Halldor Gudmund the Powerful's son had hurled the spear'

"I see him kinsman,'" said Asgrim, and then he shot a spear at Skapti, and struck him just below where the calf was fattest'

'Flosi threw a spear at Bruni Haflidi's son, and caught him at the waist'

'...a spear was hurled out of the band of Gudmund the Powerful, and it struck Ljot in the middle, and he fell down dead at once'

'...and snatched a spear from a man, and hurled it at Eyjolf, and it struck him in the waist, and went through him, and Eyjolf then fell dead to earth'

VIII

'A labouring thrall came running to the river-side, and threw a hay-fork into their troop. It struck the king on the head, so that he fell instantly from his horse and died'

XI

'Others again say that nobody could tell who shot the king, which is indeed the most likely; for spears, arrows, and all kinds of missiles flew as thick as a snow-drift'

XIII

'So many spears were thrown against Earl Hakon that his armour was altogether split asunder, and he threw it off'

'The king stood on the gangways of the Long Serpent and shot the greater part of the day; sometimes with the bow, sometimes with the spear, and always throwing two spears at once'

XVI

'...but when they had broken their shield-rampart the Englishmen rode up from all sides, and threw arrows and spears on them'

✧ CATCHING THE SPEAR AND THROWING IT BACK

This is the technique of tracking a spear mid-flight, snatching it from its trajectory and then returning the spear to its sender or simply discarding it. It is probable that training

After catching a spear, the fighter must then turn it around and pick a target to launch it at, this may not be the original thrower.

THE ILLUSTRATED GUIDE TO VIKING MARTIAL ARTS

repetition was required to become an adept at this skill. Once one has practised first, facing the thrown spear and moving out of the way, it is best to then move to slapping the thrown spear out of the air and eventually catching the thrown spear. Through this training you come to realise that this is by no means a fantastical skill and is in fact quite practical in execution.

Saga References

Historically this has been recorded in other cultures. It is a skill attributed to Celtic or Iron Age warriors and can be seen in the histories and contemporary fighting arts called 'Lua', the warrior way of the Hawaiian people. Modern documentary evidence has shown these warrior people catching and throwing back not only a single spear but a succession of them. There is a custom of throwing a spear at a visiting tribal chief with the purpose of him catching it and showing his prowess.

VII

'Kari ran his ship alongside the other side of Gunnar's ship, and hurled a spear athwart the deck, and aimed at him about the waist. Gunnar sees this, and turned him about so quickly that no eye could follow him, and caught the spear with his left hand, and hurled it back at Karli's ship, and that man got his death who stood before it'

'Audulf the Easterling snatches up a spear and launches it at Gunnar. Gunnar caught the spear with his hand in the air, and hurled it back at once, and it flew through the shield and the Easterling too, and so down into the earth'

'Now Kari turns to meet Earl Melsnati, and Melsnati hurled a spear at him, but Kari caught the spear and threw it back and through the earl'

'Grani Gunnar's son snatched up a spear and hurled it at Kari, but Kari thrust down his shield so hard that the point stood fast in the ground, but with his left hand he caught the spear in the air, and hurled it back at Grani, and caught up his shield again at once with his left hand'

✧ THE THRUST

This is without doubt the primary attack of the spear in the Viking world; it constitutes most of the spear references from the sagas researched. Because of the volume of material on the thrust the different versions will be dealt with under a few headings. These include thrusts that are low-level, high-level, upward, double- and single-handed. This section will deal with only the basic 'Mid-level Thrust'.

Saga References

It appears that when a thrust strikes true and causes damage it does so with a devastating effect. The sagas sometimes claim that a thrust can pierce shield and man and that most

Version 1: The double handed mid-level thrust.

Version 2: The single handed mid-level thrust with shield.

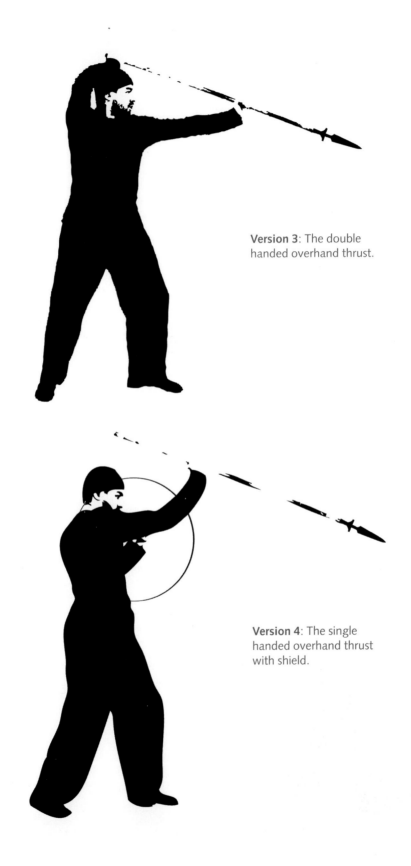

Version 3: The double handed overhand thrust.

Version 4: The single handed overhand thrust with shield.

result in either a great wound or a dead opponent. In the first quotation, the attacker strikes with the end of a staff, not a spear.

IV

'…and sprang up and drove at him with the staff so that he fell stunned'

'Now when Snorri and his folk came to the garth, it is not told that any words befell there, but straightway they set on Arnkel, and chiefly with spear-thrust'

'Thorleif took a spear which stood there in the doorway, and thrust it at Thord'

'…and the thrust smote his shield and glanced off it unto the shoulder, and that was a great wound'

'…and would thrust at Thorleif Kimbi with a spear'

'He took his weapons and went after them, and came up with them west of Svelgriver twixt it and the Knolls, but as soon as he came up with them, Hawk leapt off his horse and thrust at Arnkel with a spear, and smote his shield, yet he gat no wound. Then Arnkel sprang from his horse and thrust with a spear at Hawk, and smote him in the midst, and he fell there on the place which is now called Hawks-river'

V

'At this brunt Helgi, the son of Hardbein, rushed in with a spear, the head of which was an ell long, and the shaft bound with iron'

'Helgi thrust at Bolli with the spear right through the shield and through him'

VI

'At that moment Grettir returned, and taking his halberd in both hands he thrust it right through Thorir's body just as he was about to descend the steps. The blade was very long and broad. Ogmund the Bad was just behind pushing him on, so that the spear passed right up to the hook, came out at his back between the shoulder blades and entered the breast of Ogmund. They both fell dead, pierced by the spear'

'It was raining hard, so he did not go outside, but stood holding both the door-posts with his hands and peering round. At that moment Thorbjorn sidled round to the front of the door and thrust his spear with both hands into Atli's middle, so that it pierced him through. Atli said when he received the thrust: 'They use broad spear-blades nowadays.''

VII

'Auzur turns to meet him, and thrust at him, but fell down full length on his back, for another man thrust at him'

'Gunnar's shield was just before the boom, and Hallgrim thrust his bill into it'

'After that Atli thrust at him with his spear, and struck him about his middle'

'Sigmund had a helm on his head, and a shield at his side, and was girt with a sword, his spear was in his hand; now he turns against Skarphedinn, and thrusts at once at him with his spear, and the thrust came on his shield'

'…but Helgi thrust him through with his spear, and he got his death there and then'

'…and as he said this he thrust at Gunnar with a great spear which he held in both hands'

'With that he rushes at Gunnar in great wrath, and thrust his spear through his shield, and so on through his arm'

'Thorgrim the Easterling went and began to climb up on the hall; Gunnar sees that a red kirtle passed before the windowslit, and thrusts out the bill, and smote him on the middle'

'Then the Vikings shot at them and the fight began, and the chapmen guard themselves well. Snowcolf sprang aboard and at Olaf, and thrust his spear through his body, but Grim thrust at Snowcolf with his spear, and so stoutly, that he fell overboard'

'Just then Helgi and Grim came up both to meet Kari, and Helgi springs on Gritgard and thrusts his spear through him, and that was his death blow'

As can be seen, an 'Upward Thrust' could be at any angle that the fighter required.

'…and so here an end shall be put to it,' says Grim; and with that he ran him through with a spear, and then Hrapp fell down dead'

'There he met Grim the Red, Flosi's kinsman, and as soon as ever they met, Thorhall thrust at him with the spear, and smote him on the shield and clove it in twain, but the spear passed right through him, so that the point came out between his shoulders'

XIII

'Then Thorer Hund struck at him with his spear, and the stroke went in under his mail-coat and into his belly'

✧ THE UPWARD THRUST

This is a spear thrust that is executed from an angle that aims at the opponent's head and then through other angles upwards until one even reaches a vertical strike. The need for such a wide range of 'Upward Thrusts' can be seen from the situations within the sagas. Again, this can be done one- or two-handed.

Saga References

In all of these following situations the need for this technique is derived from an opponent being on higher ground; we can conclude this because most thrusts were to the stomach area.

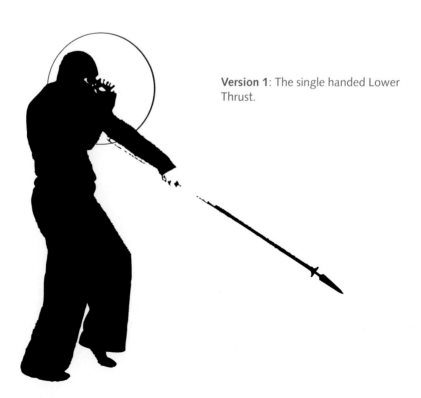

Version 1: The single handed Lower Thrust.

Version 2: The double handed Lower Thrust.

IV

'…and when they came to the homestead they leapt off their horses and were minded to enter, but might not break open the door. Then they leapt up on to the house, and fell to unroofing it … Arnbiorn took his weapons, and warded himself from the inside of the house. He thrust out through the thatch, and that became woundsome to them.'

V

'…and forthwith Helgi thrust his spear out through the window and through Hrapp, so that he fell dead to earth from the spear'

'Hardbein thrust a halberd out through where the door was broken, and the thrust struck the steel cap of Thorstein the Black and stuck in his forehead, and that was a very great wound'

VI

'Seeing that they could do nothing, they sprang on to the roof and began to break it in. Then Grettir got on to his feet, seized a spear and thrust it between the rafters'

✧ THE LOWER THRUST

This is a thrust that is aimed between the hips and the feet with the intention of wounding the opponent, it is not likely that one would sustain a death wound from such a stroke and so is reaction to an opening in the opponent's defence. This move can be done either one- or two-handed.

Saga References

Wounds created by this strike would – if the sufferer survived the battle – cause lasting damage. A wound could either become infected or could cripple a warrior.

IV

'Then Snorri the Priest went thereto, and felt along his leg, and found a spear stuck through his leg between the hough sinew and the leg bone, that had nailed together the leg and the breeches'

V

'So Lambi made a thrust at him in the thigh, and a great wound that was'

VII

'Kol thrust at him with his spear; Kolskegg had just slain a man and had his hands full, and so he could not throw his shield before the blow, and the thrust came upon his thigh, on the outside of the limb and went through it'

XVII

'King Magnus received a wound, being pierced by a spear through both thighs above the knees'

✧ THE IMPALE AND LIFT

The opponent is impaled after a 'Mid-Level Thrust' and then using his momentum is lifted into the air and then smashed into the ground. The technique involved in this movement would exploit the energy of the opponent's attack and the spear would be braced against the ground. It was finished with a single huge burst of strength.

Saga References

This, out of all the techniques investigated here, is probably the most unbelievable. However, that being said and with the understanding that the audience for both the oral and the written form of the sagas was well versed in combat, we can hope to find some

truth here. People of the medieval world were, if only slightly, smaller then those of today, most would have been slim. In addition, we simply cannot comprehend the strength of someone who has worked all of their lives in a medieval setting. Take, for example, the colossal power of the draw on an English medieval longbow and the rarity of men today who can replicate such a feat of strength. Even at a later date, consider the unfeasible weight of Henry VIII's armour. Thinking of a Viking as a person who, from a walking age, worked a farm, pulled an oar, drew the bow, lifted ships and sailed the north seas, we can start to understand that the act of simply lifting another human in the air may not be such an extraordinary feat after all. For are these not the elite warriors of the north?

VII

'Gunnar gives another thrust with his bill, and through Skamkell, and lifts him up and casts him down in the muddy path on his head'

Version 1: 'The Slash ad Cut' could be made overhead and be delivered to the opponent's head, face or shoulders.

Version 2: 'The Slash and Cut' could be made from a sideways angle and be delivered to the opponent's head, body or legs.

'But when Egil sees this, he runs at Gunnar and makes a cut at him; Gunnar thrusts at him with the bill and struck him in the middle, and Gunnar hoists him up on the bill and hurls him out into Rangriver'

'Thorgeir Otkell's son had come near him with a drawn sword, and Gunnar turns on him in great wrath, and drives the bill through him, and lifts him up aloft, and casts him out into Rangriver'

'Just then Thorbrand Thorleik's son, sprang up on the roof, and cuts asunder Gunnar's bowstring. Gunnar clutches the bill with both hands, and turns on him quickly and drives it through him, and hurls him down on the ground'

✧ THE SLASH AND CUT

This is of course the process of making a cut in an arc from side to side or up and down as opposed to a thrust with the point. This would have been with the intention of delivering either a bludgeoning blow with the iron spearhead or to cut or lacerate the opponent if the spearhead was sharp enough.

Saga References

We can speculate by reference to other martial arts that if a spear is touching the exposed parts of the enemy's skin then the spear-man could rapidly draw the weapon

along the exposed flesh, using his own motion to cut from a stationary point; this might have happened when combat had become congested and the spear blade was resting on exposed skin. It is an opportunistic strike.

VI

'On Grettir entering the giant sprang up, seized a pike and struck at him, for he could both strike and thrust with it'

VII

'There lay a pole-axe in the corner of the dais. Asgrim caught it up with both hands, and ran up to the rail at the edge of the dais, and made a blow at Flosi's head' [this could be a thrust]

✧ THE STRIKE TO THE CENTRE OF THE BACK

This is a cut or thrust that appears quite often in the literature of the sagas. The point of entry is described as being between the shoulder blades and presumably on the spine. It is sometimes executed as a thrust and at other times it is unclear if it is a cut. The attack is usually done with a spear or other pole-arm. It is probable that this would have only mainly been a forward stepping attack as it would need power to work its way through cloth or armour. The thrust is a more likely candidate for the attacking style, however, this

The unsuspecting opponent receives his death-wound in the back.

does not rule out the cut version. This is an attack that also usually ends in the death of the opponent or if not it still creates damage. There seems to be no stigma attached to striking the enemy in the back during a 'fair fight'.

Saga References

This appears to be a killing stroke and usually ends in the opponent's death; however as we can see in the second quote, even a miss can result in serious damage to an opponent.

I

'As soon as Vali saw them he turned and hewed at Bersi. Halldor came at his back and fleshed Whitting in his hough-sinews. Thereupon he turned sharply and fell upon Halldor. Then Bersi set the halberd-point betwixt his shoulders. That was his death-wound'

IV

'…but Mar Hallwardson came next, and Swart thrust the bill at him, and it smote the shoulder-blade, and glanced off out towards the armpit, and there cut itself through'

V

'…and when Hrut saw that, he raised up his halberd and struck Eidgrim through the back between the shoulders'

VI

'Thorbjorn Angle was able to wound him severely between the shoulders'

5

THE AXE

The axe is of course the most iconic weapon of the Vikings. The bearded image of a wild man with an axe almost too big to wield, the 'berserker', is forever in our minds. This unrealistic image is slowly being replaced by a more accurate picture. However, one element of the old fearful image has to stay, and that is the sheer power of a Viking axe and the damage it can inflict upon the human body, upon armour and shield.

This chapter proves more complex then the sword or spear sections before it. With a sword or a spear one knows what type of weapon one is dealing with. The axe on the other hand can be in various forms, from the adze working tool to the small wood-chopping version, to a thrown weapon and then to the mighty war, or great, axe. When the text does not specify which axe is in use the readers finds themselves having to work it out from the situation. Therefore, while most images in this section portray a single axe, the reader must remember the various types.

The axe is not a slow weapon, in fact the concept of a slow weapon is a ridiculous notion from the start – what warrior would even contemplate using something that would only lead to their death? Unless he was ordered to do so by an incompetent military hierarchy – and there are plenty of examples of that throughout history. The Vikings had no such top-down organisation, one of the reasons they were such formidable foes. The Dane axe, or hafted axe, most popular during the transition from the European Viking Age to the early Middle Ages, weighed only 1 or 2 kg and was incredibly sharp. That being said, a top-heavy weapon, while fast in the hands of an expert, will not have the same potential speed as the sword.

✧ THE OVERHEAD CUT

This is a basic cutting action that can be found in all martial arts across the world. It has the primary target of the head with the intent of splitting the opponent's skull and is to be considered to be a lethal cut in all its applications. With the axe, several variations were available, a double-handed axe, for example, will have differing dynamics to a single-handed axe. As with the sword, the use of a double-handed axe would have meant that a fighter would have to attack from a slightly longer distance and therefore a straightforward step and cut would have taken place. On the other hand, the single-handed axe would have been used more 'up close and personal' and the cut may have been produced by dropping the hips more than actually a full step and cut.

The basic 'Overhead Cut' with a larger axe.

Saga References

The archaeological finds concerned with any period of medieval combat show a variety of angles of cut into the skull and this should be remembered here more than anywhere else. You might consider the 'Overhead Cut' to be within the range of perhaps 40 degrees either side of the crown, down to the side of the jaw and on both sides.

IV

> 'Now Arnkel fell to boring holes in the door-ledge, and laid his adze down the while. Thorleif took it up, and heaved it up swiftly over his head with the mind to bring it down on Arnkel's skull'

A double-handed axe would need a step to really generate power behind the cut. Remembering that dynamic motion is three-dimensional and that a transfer of movement from the hips to axe is what delivers true power.

'…and the adze flew out of his hand, and Arnkel got hold thereof and smote it into Thorleif's head, and gave him his death-wound'

VI

'One day Grettir and Arnbjorn were walking along the road for their diversion when they passed a gate, whence a man rushed out holding an axe aloft with both hands and struck at Grettir'

VII

'Aunund of Witchwood smote the hound on the head with his axe, so that the blade sunk into the brain. The hound gave such a great howl that they thought it passing strange, and he fell down dead'

'Thrain was just about to put his helm on his head; and now Skarphedinn bore down on them, and hews at Thrain with his axe, 'the ogress of war,' and smote him on the head, and clove him down to the teeth, so that his jaw-teeth fell out on the ice'

'With that he ran straight into the booth until he comes before Lyting, and smites him with an axe on the head, so that it sunk in up to the hammer, and gives the axe a pull towards him'

'Thorgeir lifted the axe, 'the ogress of war,' with both hands, and dashed the hammer of the axe with a back-blow into the head of him that stood behind him, so that his skull was shattered to small bits'

XIV

'Thord the Low seized the stick-axe, which lay in the field at his side, and struck the axe-blade right into Karl's skull'

XV

'Asmund struck Harek on the head, so that the axe penetrated to the brains; and that was Harek's death-wound'

XVIII

'Then he heaved his axe forwards, and struck the next man in the head, and clove him down to the shoulders'

✧ THE STRIKE TO THE NECK

This is a cut with an axe with the aim of either cleaving through the jaw, neck and collar bone or with the intention of decapitation. Like the similar cut with the sword, this is closely linked with a 'High-level Horizontal Cut' to the neck. For categorisation purposes here we will class this as a downward stroke at any of the varying angles between vertical and horizontal. Again, as with the sword, this could be done on either the left or the right side of the opponent.

Saga References

The fact that not all human targets are standing in an upright position when the cuts are made is often overlooked and here we see a prime example. The third quotation here displays what is in fact an 'Overhead Cut' as the berserker is actually falling from his horse.

V

'Then Steinthor Olafson leapt at Bolli, and hewed at his neck with a large axe just above his shoulders, and forthwith his head flew off'

VI

'"Here I bring you your axe," said Thorgeir. Then he struck at Thorfinn's neck and cut off his head'

This time, the stroke is illustrated by using a small axe and shield – note the different area of attack and damage.

'With the same movement he seized the Viking's helmet with his left hand and dragged him from his horse, while with his right hand he raised his axe and cut off the berserker's head'

XVII

'A little after King Magnus was struck in the neck with an Irish axe, and this was his death-wound'

XVIII

'Olver lifted his axe, and struck behind him with the extreme point of it, hitting the neck of the man who was coming up behind him, so that his throat and jawbone were cut through, and he fell dead backwards'

✧ STRIKING THE SHOULDER

Hitting downwards in an angled arc with the intention of taking off the arm of the opponent or shattering the shoulder joint and area. This strike can be done on either the left of the right side with the intention of hitting the opponent on either shoulder.

Saga References

There are references to a tug after an axe has embedded in the opponent with the intention of bringing them down. Looking here at the second quotation one can see the axe-man pulling the foe off balance once the axe has been driven in. He would have used the power from the hips for the pull, not the strength of his arm. The shape of the bearded axe, with its pronounced hook, or 'beard', meant that it could have been used to pull shields or weapons out of the hands of an opponent without an actual strike.

VII

'Thiostolf cut at him at once with his axe, and smote him on the shoulder, and the stroke hewed asunder the shoulder-bone and collarbone, and the wound bled inwards'

'Then Skarphedinn hews at Sigmund with his axe; the "Ogress of war". Sigmund had on a corselet, the axe came on his shoulder. Skarphedinn cleft the shoulder-blade right through, and at the same time pulled the axe towards him. Sigmund fell down on both knees, but sprang up again at once'

'But when he dashed the axe forward, he smote Thorkell on the shoulder, and hewed it off, arm and all'

The same strike but this time illustrated from the rear – however, this time the wounded man has damage to the other shoulder, to show that attacks can come on both sides.

XIV

'Thorer struck a blow with the hammer of it on the shoulder so hard that he tottered'

✧ THE SHIELD CLEAVE

Strangely, there does not seem to be any references to a 'Lower Shield Cleave' unlike the sword. The shield cleave is an attack to the shoulder but aimed at the shield itself.

Saga References

VII

'[He] lifts up his axe and hews at Sigmund, and cleaves his shield down to below the handle'

'Thorgeir had hewn with the "Ogress of war", holding it with both hands, and the lower horn fell on the shield and clove it in twain, but the upper caught the collarbone and cut it in two and tore on down into the breast and trunk'

✧ THE HORIZONTAL CUT

This, like its sword counterpart, is a horizontal strike to either side of the body with the intention of cutting open the opponent or to stun him if the back of the axe is used.

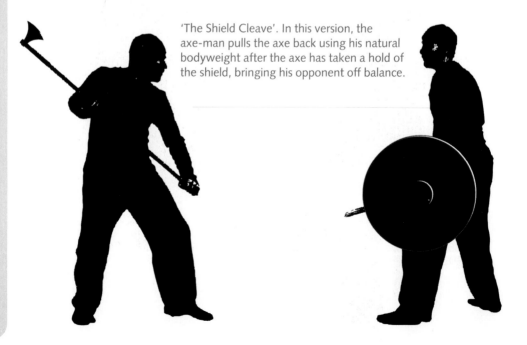

'The Shield Cleave'. In this version, the axe-man pulls the axe back using his natural bodyweight after the axe has taken a hold of the shield, bringing his opponent off balance.

Version 1: 'The Horizontal Cut'. This double-handed strike is executed with a stepping motion to any area of the body on one side. It is most unlikely that anyone would use a shield whilst using a larger axe.

Version 2: The 'Horizontal Cut' with the single-handed axe would be a much more 'snappy' effort, where the aim would be to strike out quickly and then to return to the shelter of the shield.

Saga References

One must remember that while chain mail does offer some protection it is almost redundant against an axe, as an axe relies on its weight and bludgeoning power as much as its cutting power.

IV

'Uspak turned to meet him and fetched a blow at him with his axe-hammer, and smote him on the ear so that he fell swooning'

'The Mid-level Strike to the Legs' with a step to supply power to the blow.

V

'Hunbogi the Strong went to meet Thorgils, and dealt a blow at him with an axe, and it struck the back of him, and cut him asunder in the middle'

VII

'Skarphedinn made a side blow at him with his axe, the "Ogress of war", and hews asunder his backbone'

✧ THE MID-LEVEL STRIKE TO THE LEGS

This is a swinging arc attack to the body, delivered between the hips and the knee joint with the intention to sever or break the legs. Axe size and weight is important here, it seems unlikely that a small axe would cause more then superficial damage in comparison with the war axe, depending on the armour. Though an unprotected leg would still receive a terrible blow. Therefore, here we assume the larger of the axe family is employed and concentrate on two elements: the strike itself and return of the axe.

Saga Reference

XIV

'Thorstein Knarrarsmid struck at King Olaf with his axe, and the blow hit his left leg above the knee'

The return of the axe to its starting position from a missed strike to the legs – to do this, the attacker must allow the axe to continue on its path and let go with his right hand. The axe will continue to swing in his left, and he can permit it to go upwards and return to the starting position.

✧ ATTACKING THE FEET WITH A THROWN AXE

The axe (or any other projectile) is thrown downward with the intention of wounding or penetrating the opponent's foot to cripple them and take them out of the fight. Delivering this blow accurately is not impossible but it is difficult, so it would appear logical that this strike was an effective distraction to gain advantage. If the strike did hit the target all the better, if not the fighter could still be upon his opponent with his other weapon. Once the weapon has left the hand it is forgotten about.

Saga Reference

Interestingly, we tend to see the small axe as a primarily a throwing weapon. Perhaps this is because of our seeing the Native American tomahawk thrown in films and fictional Vikings following suit. However, there is little evidence from these sagas to show that the Vikings were throwing these axes apart from the following.

V

'…and therewith he flung the axe at Thorgils, and the axe struck his foot, and a great wound that was'

✧ ATTACKING THE ARMS

Again, this move would depend upon a set of variables such as position of attack, type of axe used and whether one defended from the inside or outside. The images here are of a basic attack that represents a multitude of possibilities.

Saga References

As the sword blow could cut the arm clean off or result in deep laceration wounds, the axe could deliver a crushing blow that would break the arm or joints. Note that in the second quotation the victim is armed with an axe, so the attack could be launched against any type of weapon.

VII

'Then Thorwald snatched up a fishing-knife that lay by him, and made a stab at Thiostolf; he had lifted his axe to his shoulder and dashed it down. It came on Thorwald's arm and crushed the wrist, but down fell the knife. Then Thiostolf lifted up his axe a second time and gave Thorwald a blow on the head, and he fell dead on the spot'

'Helgi sees this and cuts at Hrapp's arm, and cut it off, and down fell the axe'

THE AXE

Having the axe in hand, he steps forward and throws the axe with a flick, then instantly follows up with a second attack. This could be done by having a sword in the left hand while throwing the axe with the right, which would then require the fighter to move the sword over to the right hand or strike left-handed, or to have the ability to throw with the left hand. This strike is to open a window of opportunity and force the opponent to make a move. Even if they only have to move out of the way of the thrown axe, that still produces openings, meaning that the thrown axe itself does not have to hit, the goal is to create movement in the opponent.

Similar to the dismembering of the hand with a sword, this is the same concept with the axe. In the second image, the man on the left has aimed for the forearm of the opponent's attacking limb and severed the hand from the arm, which allows him to follow up with a smashing blow to the face, which in turn will open up a window of opportunity for a killing blow. Complete dismemberment with an axe might seem less likely than with a sword, but one must remember that the axe blade was honed to an extreme sharpness.

In this scenario, the fighter has hit the opponent's axe haft with his own haft, causing the attacking weapon to bounce backwards, which will allow him to follow up with an attack.

✧ SUNDERING A WEAPON

Sundering a weapon with an axe is the process of making a strike at the same time as your opponent with the intent of hitting his weapon or around the area of his hands or the haft, to dislodge his weapon or to break it.

Saga Reference

In the Japanese sword arts there is a concept of striking at the same time and it is the nerve of the swordsman that gains him victory. We see here that a similar understanding must have been had, for if the Viking missed his strike to the haft of the opponents' weapon then he would be left open and in the path of a possibly mortal blow.

'Brynjolf rode at Thord, and smote at him with his axe. He smote at him at the same time with his axe, and hewed in sunder the haft just above Brynjolf's hands, and then hewed at him at once a second time, and struck him on the collar-bone, and the blow went straight into his trunk. Then he fell from horseback, and was dead on the spot'

✧ THE PARRY AND CUT

This is striking the blade of the opponent's weapon to deflect their attack to one side and thus opening a window for you to attack. Like the sword parry in the last chapter, you should not view this as the 'graceful' flick of modern fencing but as a strike in itself, a blow aginst the opponents' blade. This is then followed up by any attack that is open after the parry has been completed.

This parry can be in multiple directions, be it from the outside or the inside and would be followed up by an attack to any opening. Note that this situation is the reverse of the saga quotation to show that it can work both ways, here the swordsman is parrying the axe strike.

THE AXE

Saga Reference

The reference states the size of his axe and that the axe-man is up against a sword. For a modern reinterpreter of historical martial arts it is of great interest to find confirmation that a large axe could be handled with speed and accuracy. Historical martial reconstructors know that the swords and the large axes of western traditions were not slow and unwieldy. The larger weapons must have been slower, but the difference would have been fractions of a second as opposed to the lumbering depictions of Hollywood. It is satisfying to find a reference to a large axe used in a fluid and speedy way against the sword.

XIII

> 'He had a large axe; and when Alfvine was going to cut at him with his sword, he hewed away the sword out of his hand, and with the next blow struck down Alfvine himself'

✧ AMBIDEXTERITY

In this case being ambidextrous does not actually mean, say, being able to switch a sword from one hand to the other with equal facility, it means having a weapon in each hand and being able to use them in such a manner that one is competent enough to trust one's life to the skill. The two main questions which arise are 'which hand holds which weapon?' and 'did the Vikings use a shield with this form of fighting?'

A combination of fighting with the spear and sword is recorded. Here we see that the sword is in the left hand: 'He had a spear in one hand, and a sword in the other … Thrust with the right hand … With his left hand he made a cut at Mord, and smote him on the hip.'

The answer to the first, maybe both questions seems given; however, there are other factors. Is this example the norm, does this change from case to case and does the man mentioned have a dominant right or left hand? We can only guess but we can say with a degree of certainty that the man in the example has a much higher chance of being right-handed then left. Therefore, we will take the following on trust. When a Viking wielded a set of weapons he did so with the sword in his left hand and the spear in his right and that it was probably reversed for a left-handed person. This is speculative. [As a left-hander and imagining the threat of death, I'm not entirely convinced! Though closing distance and speed would no doubt be a crucial factor. Ed.] The main point here is the ability to switch effectively between weapons.

The second question, did a Viking use a shield when he had two weapons, is also tricky. Logically one would say, no, as it would be cumbersome. However, there is a quotation that opens up the question: 'He had a spear in one hand, and a sword in the other, but no shield.' Why tell us if it was the norm? It is almost impossible to use a sword effectively with a shield in the same hand. However, it is possible to thrust with a spear whilst your forearm supports the shield. We tentatively conclude:

- The Vikings could wield two weapons at once
- They were predominantly the spear and the sword
- It is possible that a shield was used at the same time; however, it would have had to have been with the spear hand so that one could thrust and shield.

Version 1: These two images show the Viking holding the weapons in the manner described.

Version 2: The first saga quotation describes moving the sword from hand to hand. If ever done in reality, it was most likely to try to make an opening in the opponent, partly through distraction.

Saga References

The first quotation below is intriguing; one can see the advantages of changing sword hands during a fight, but to do it before the combat begins must be a distraction, an attempt to open a gap or simply to intimidate.

I

'Then Ogmund whirled about his sword swiftly and shifted it from hand to hand'

VII

'Then I took my sword, and I smote with it with one hand, but thrust at them with my bill with the other'

'Then Starkad said, "Twill never answer our end that he should use his bow, but let us come on well and stoutly." Then each man egged on the other, and Gunnar guarded himself with his bow and arrows as long as he could; after that he throws them down, and then he takes his bill and sword and fights with both hands'

'Then a hard battle arose; Gunnar cut with one hand and thrust with the other. Kolskegg slew some men and wounded many'

'He had a spear in one hand, and a sword in the other, but no shield. He thrust with the right hand at Sigmund Sigfus' son, and smote him on his breast, and the spear came out between his shoulders, and down he fell and was dead at once. With his left hand he made a cut at Mord, and smote him on the hip, and cut it asunder, and his backbone too; he fell flat on his face, and was dead at once'

IV

'Steinthor was of the eagerest, and smote on either hand'

6

THE SHIELD

The shield is far from a static piece of Viking equipment, we see from the sagas that it was manoeuvred in a dynamic way and in ways that one would not expect. The problem with the shield is the fact that the sagas clearly describe kite shields, which probably first came into use in the late tenth century and replaced the circular shield as used by the Vikings. The tapered kite shield gave some protection to the legs without adding too much weight. One might assume that the authors of the sagas simply got it wrong, that the kite shield was anachronistic. However, it is not so clear cut, some of the events in the sagas were in the tenth century, the supposed date of entry for the kite shield. We do know that the kite shield was accepted in the Norse lands in the 12th century. The Normans are of course famed for their kite shield through its depiction in the Bayeux Tapestry and as Normans are Viking descendants, this makes the matter a little more complex.

Conifer wood such as fir was the most common material for the Viking shield. Experimental archaeology that uses what is believed to be close replica shields has shown us that:

- Viking shields were flexible, light and afforded relatively good protection
- A well placed sword blow or heavy axe could indeed cleave a shield.

It would appear that in combat the shield was used until it was rendered ineffective by blows and that a Viking would more than likely leave the fight needing a new one. We can assume that most blows were delivered to the left side of a Viking's shield. If a shield was destroyed by the end of combat a few questions arise, not necessarily germane to reconstructing the Viking martial arts but of interest nevertheless:

- Could most people make a shield?
- Was the decoration simple, as the shield would so often be destroyed?
- Did a Viking have a 'parade shield' with a high level of decoration that he used when visiting others to show status?
- Did a raiding Viking have a more simplistic shield design then a homebound farming Viking or did a raiding Viking feel decoration was a key element of his warlike presentation?

Decoration is difficult to identify from an archaeological point of view. We know that whites, yellows, reds and blues were colours used on Viking shields. Also we can gather that a spiral or spiral variation design was probably most popular. There is evidence for red being the most popular colour. With a variety of shield bosses, leather rims etc., we can only guess at the look of the shields. Archaeology cannot reveal much due to the deterioration of the wood, leather and pigment. Some saga quotations allude to decorated shields: 'Nikolas has a red shield in which were gilt nails and about it was a border of stars'; 'Sigurd Swinehead came first and had a red targe.'

Saga References

I

'Each man was allowed three shields. Bersi cut up two, and then Cormac took the third. Bersi hacked away, but Whitting his sword stuck fast in the iron border of Steinar's shield'

'When two shields had been hacked to splinters'

II

'...shields cleft and byrnies torn'

VII

'Gunnar thrust at him with his bill, and he threw his shield before the blow, but the bill passed clean through the shield and broke both his arms, and down he fell from the wall'

'Kari cut at once at him, and then a man ran forward and threw his shield before Bjarni. Kari cleft the shield in twain, and the point of the sword caught his thigh, and ripped up the whole leg down to the ankle'

✧ THE SHIELD WALL

There are not many references in the sagas to the 'Shield-wall'. This does not mean that it was not commonplace. We must consider that most of the sagas deal with individuals and their plight, or a series of individuals locked into a story. Therefore, the focus is more on individual combat.

Saga References

The shield-bearers lining the ship have a spear thrust out below their shields, as the attack would come from people trying to board the ship from below the gunwale.

II

'Tis the mind of us twain to make shields meet together' [this could mean face to face]

V

'Olaf bade the crew fetch out their weapons, and range in line of battle from stem to stern on the ship; and so thick they stood, that shield overlapped shield all round the ship, and a spear point stood out at the lower end of every shield'

Version 1: The Shield Wall with spears overhead, to be performed on both land and sea.

Version 2: The Shield Wall with spears underhand, to be performed on both land and sea but probably more likely at sea.

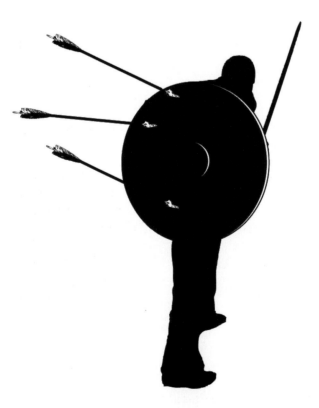

These three versions show the dynamic way a shield can be used. First, the use of the shield one-handed to catch an arrow; second, the use of the shield as a full body defence, used in both hands and finally, the use of the shield slung over the back to stop arrows when fleeing.

✧ INDIVIDUAL PROTECTION

We can see from the sagas that the shield was not static but was placed in front of blows to take the attack. Its flexibility and tendency to break may well have been deliberate, in an attempt to snare the attacker's weapon.

Saga References

It appears that the Vikings may have had the skill of deliberately catching an arrow on the shield (logically this could also be a spear; however the damage would be much greater). Even though in the quotation the man dies from the arrow piercing through the shield, we can see that he trusted the shield to hold and had the skill to catch an arrow mid-flight upon it. It brings a new element into the art of the shield. The last quotation refers to a makeshift shield of cloth wrapped around the arm, probably the cloak.

V

'When Bolli saw that he cast away his sword, and took his shield in both hands, and went towards the dairy door to meet Helgi'

VI

'Then he drew his sword and went valiantly for Grettir, who defended himself with his shield but would not use his weapons against Thorodd. They fought for a time without his being wounded'

'Illugi threw his shield before Grettir and defended him so valiantly that all men praised his prowess'

VII

'Gunnar threw his shield before the blow, but Hallbjorn pierced the shield through. Gunnar thrust the shield down so hard that it stood fast in the earth'

'Sigurd Swinehead came first and had a red target, but in his other hand he held a cutlass. Gunnar sees him and shoots an arrow at him from his bow; he held the shield up aloft when he saw the arrow flying high, and the shaft passes through the shield and into his eye, and so came out at the nape of his neck, and that was the first man slain'

'Lyting thrust at Skarphedinn, but Helgi came up then and threw his shield before the spear, and caught the blow on it'

XIII

'King Olaf threw his shield over his head, and sank beneath the waters'

XVI

'The Varings had no shields, but wrapped their cloaks round their left arms'

This is a group of men using their shields in a 'Shield Wall' formation to restrain a person for capture. It needs no explanation. However, it is interesting to see that the Vikings could act under command as a team; and that aggressive behaviour was not always responded to with equal ferocity.

Saga References

VI

'Angle then ordered them to bear Illugi down with their shields, saying he had never met with his like amongst older men than he. They did so, and pressed upon him with a wall of armour against which resistance was impossible'

This would be a twisting action and not a pulling one, the aim is to have the opponent's sword trapped in one's shield and to twist the shield to the left or to the right depending on the position of the attacker.

VII

'Then Sweyn, Earl Hacon's son, fell on them, and made men hem them in and bear them down with shields, and so they were taken captive'

✧ THE SWORD DISARM

The 'Sword Disarm' may be the most interesting technique to come out of this research, as it is a completely new element to what we believe to be western martial arts. When a Viking has received a blow to his shield and the opponent's sword has embedded in it; he would then use natural leverage and twist the shield away and disarm the opponent or break his sword.

The direction of twist would completely depend upon the direction of attack, the position of the enemy and other such factors. The most probable method would be to twist the sword against the direction of the thumb. Most martial arts that deal with wrist grabs, teach how to use natural leverage against the thumb and this is a logical step to how the Vikings may have done it.

Saga References

VII

'Against Gunnar came Vandil, and smote at once at him with his sword, and the blow fell on his shield. Gunnar gave the shield a twist as the sword pierced it, and broke it short off at the hilt'

'Sigmund drew his sword and cut at Skarphedinn, and the sword cuts into his shield, so that it stuck fast. Skarphedinn gave the shield such a quick twist, that Sigmund let go his sword'

'Gunnar gave the shield such a sharp twist that the spearhead broke short off at the socket'

✧ THE SHIELD AS A WEAPON

Here the shield is used offensively in two ways.

Saga References

In the first example we find a fleeing Viking, which runs counter to the usual concept of the Viking happy to reach Valhalla.

VII

'He glided away from them at once at full speed. Tjorvi, indeed, threw his shield before him on the ice, but he leapt over it, and still kept his feet, and slid quite to the end of the sheet of ice'

XI

'Thoralf thrust his shield so hard against Eyvind that he tottered with the shock'

Version 1: 'The Shield Throw'. It appears that the Viking did throw his shield at an enemy to hinder him, be he an oncoming attacker or in flight. Presumably, due to the size of the Viking shield, one would expect the shield to be thrown in a double-handed 'Frisbee' way, however, the only written account is of a throw at the feet and on ice.

Version 2: 'The Shield Barge' – it appears that a Viking could use his shield to smash at the opponent with the intent to shock, disorientate and open a gap in his defence. This would be done by forming a strong step with control. The image has the second hand ready to back up the thrust, as how we would follow up would depend on what the fighter had as a weapon in hand. Also, the attacker would have to be careful not to lean too far forward lest his opponent let him fall through his own momentum.

✧ THE REDIRECTION

The 'Redirection' is the process of aligning the shield so that the blow given by the opponent glances off. The physical method would depend upon the angle of attack, but is always designed to open a window of opportunity for a counter strike. The deflection would differ greatly depending on if the attack is made by a spear, sword or axe.

The swordsman on the left has used his shield to deflect the opponent's sword blow downwards and towards the attacker's left, leaving the right side of the man exposed for a counter strike.

Saga References

Here the reality of combat with a shield as more dynamic and fluid than one might expect is clearest. The shield does not block a blow, it deflects it purposefully.

VII

'Kari Solmund's son came up where Bjarni Broddhelgi's son had the lead. Kari caught up a spear and thrust at him, and the blow fell on his shield. Bjarni slipped the shield on one side of him, else it had gone straight through him'

'Then Lambi Sigfus' son rushed at Kari, and hewed at him with his sword. Kari caught the blow sideways on his shield, and the sword would not bite'

✧ KNOCKING DOWN A SPEAR

This was a perhaps surprisingly necessary skill – until you remember the 'Shield Wall'.

It is probable that a spear in full flight would pierce a shield, therefore, if confident of his skills, a swordsman could knock the spear out of the air with the rim instead of letting it impact on the surface.

Saga Reference

We know catching a spear in flight is not only possible but also historically proven, so to execute this move is not so remarkable. That being said, why would a Viking do this instead of simply moving out of the way? Or why not simply take the hit on the shield? Firstly, a Viking may be fighting in a shield wall or a troop and cannot simply sidestep. Secondly, we know that a spear throw had great penetrative power and the Viking would not wish to risk impalement. Further, we have to consider the mores of a warrior culture based on prestige and status as won by martial prowess. The warrior who can display high-level skills in a life-and-death situation gains a higher status (and strikes fear in the enemy); and this gives him such an opportunity.

VII

'Grani Gunnar's son snatched up a spear and hurled it at Kari, but Kari thrust down his shield so hard that the point stood fast in the ground'

7

UNARMED COMBAT

Unarmed combat is by far the most complex area that this book has to deal with. Writing an accurate description of unarmed combat is difficult even today. It is virtually impossible to accurately describe the subtleties of the flow of dynamic movements that occur between two or more people. The descriptions here are being written down 200 years later and possibly by a non-combatant. Though they were written in a warrior culture and for an audience of people that would be used to combat. With weaponry it is easy to describe the movements, such as decapitating blows, cuts to legs and thrusts through the body, because they are defined by the weapon. What we can gain from the quotations is that unarmed combat was harsh, fast and destructive.

The words 'unarmed combat' refer to fighting without implements designed for war. In the ancient world, truly unarmed combat only arose when it was competitive. In real life situations, during this period, unarmed combat as we know it did not exist. Most of the time a weapon is at hand, if not, then an improvised implement is to be had. One must not confuse sport combat with historic fighting. One is purely a sport, the other a fight to the death with anything to hand.

Talhoffer's fifteenth-century fight book shows the types of wrestling popular in medieval Europe.

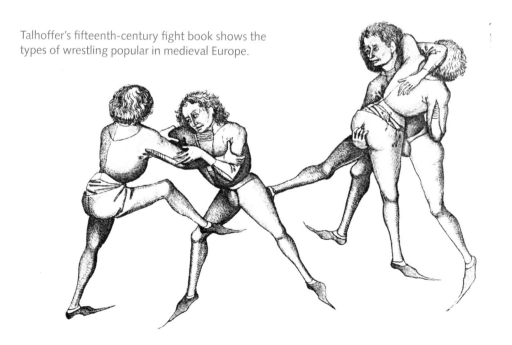

✧ THE BODY GRAPPLE

For the 'Body Grapple' we can assume that the two combatants gripped each other upon the shoulders and arms, which we know to be a medieval style of wrestling. From this initial grab we can expect that the two combatants tried to find weaknesses in the other by the use of holds and throws in what appears to be a strength and skills orientated match. However, it simply may be a later writer's interpretation of what 'Unarmed Combat' appeared to be like. There are no punches thrown in the sagas.

Saga References

Tables, doors and furniture are smashed. These are not boxing matches.

IV

'Now Arnkel fell to boring holes in the door-ledge, and laid his adze down the while. Thorleif took it up, and heaved it up swiftly over his head with the mind to bring it down on Arnkel's skull, but Arnkel heard the whistle of it and ran in under the stroke, and heaved up Thorleif by the breast, and soon was proven the measure of either's strength, for Arnkel was wondrous strong. So he cast Thorleif down with so great a fall that he lay stunned, and the adze flew out of his hand, and Arnkel got hold thereof and smote it into Thorleif's head, and gave him his death-wound'

V

'Grim sprang forthwith upon Thorkell, and they seized each other wrestling-wise, and speedily the odds of strength told, and Thorkell fell and Grim on the top of him'

VI

'Grettir took all the treasure and went back towards the rope, but on his way he felt himself seized by a strong hand. He left the treasure to close with his aggressor and the two engaged in a merciless struggle. Everything about them was smashed'

'Soon they came to the place where the horse's bones were lying, and here they struggled for long, each in turn being brought to his knees'

'Suddenly Grettir sprang under his arms, seized him round the waist and squeezed his back with all his might, intending in that way to bring him down, but the thrall wrenched his arms till he staggered from the violence. Then Grettir fell back to another bench. The benches flew about and everything was shattered around them. Glam wanted to get out, but Grettir tried to prevent him by stemming his foot against anything he could find. Nevertheless Glam succeeded in getting him outside the hall...Then Glam made a desperate effort and gripped Grettir tightly towards him, forcing him to the porch. Grettir saw that he could not put up any resistance, and with a sudden movement he dashed into the thrall's arms and set both his feet against a stone which was fastened in the ground at the door. For that Glam was not prepared, since he had been tugging to drag Grettir towards him; he reeled backwards and tumbled hind-foremost out of the door, tearing away the lintel with his shoulder and shattering the roof, the rafters and the frozen thatch…What with fatigue and all else that he had endured, when he saw the horrible rolling of Glam's eyes [Grettir's] heart sank so utterly that he had not strength to draw his sword, but lay there wellnigh betwixt life and death. Glam possessed more malignant power than most fiends'

✧ THE MANIPULATIVE GRAB

As with the description of unarmed combat, the manipulative grab is very difficult to describe. All that can be said is that grabbing the clothes of another and then manipulating *their* movement can result in the combatant ending up in a stronger position. This is of course a technique everyone recognises from Judo.

Saga Reference

IV

'Such hasty rede took Biorn that he caught up the knife and turned swiftly to meet them, and when he came up to Snorri he caught hold of the sleeve of his cape with one hand, and held the knife in the other, in such wise as it was handiest to thrust it into Snorri's breast if need should be'

✧ THE IMPROVISED WEAPON

What can be noted from the text is the frequent use of non-weapon objects to attack. Two Vikings would literally take anything to hand and smash it against the opponent with the aim of bludgeoning them and winning the fight. There is simply no methodology in this and each case is dependent upon what the improvised weapon of choice was.

Saga References

Of all the quotes dealing with improvised weaponry none is more awe-inspiring than the berserker having his jaw broken with his own shield and then being taken from the saddle and decapitated. It is images like this that show that in Viking forms of battlefield combat any way of killing was accepted.

VI

'The berserker thought they were trying to get off by talking. He began to howl and to bite the rim of his shield. He held the shield up to his mouth and scowled over its upper edge like a madman. Grettir stepped quickly across the ground, and when he got even with the berserker's horse he kicked the shield with his foot from below with such force that it struck his mouth, breaking the upper jaw, and the lower jaw fell down on to his chest. With the same movement he seized the Viking's helmet with his left hand and dragged him from his horse, while with his right hand he raised his axe and cut off the berserker's head'

This situation has been adapted here to ground combat. The principle remains the same, to smash the opponent's jaw by kicking the lower rim of the shield.

'Leif beat one of Steinn's men to death with a rib of the whale'

'Six of the ruffians fell, all slain by Grettir's own hand; the other six then fled towards the landing place and took refuge in the boat-house, where they defended themselves with oars. Grettir received a severe blow from one of them and narrowly escaped a serious hurt'

'Then all the others dashed down as they reached the steps. Grettir tackled them each in turn, now thrusting with the spear, now hewing with the sword, while they defended themselves with logs lying on the ground or with anything else which they could get. It was a terrible trial of a man's prowess to deal with men of their strength, even unarmed'

VII

'Thangbrand smote the arm of the Baresark with his crucifix, and so mighty a token followed that the sword fell from the Baresark's hand'

✧ THE THROW

This is a heavily debated subject in the world of martial arts and the difference between a 'physical throw' such as in Judo versus a dynamic and 'effortless throw' such as Akido is a popular subject. Remembering all the problematic issues that surround interpreting 'Unarmed Combat' we would suspect that the throwing style of the Vikings would focus on 'physical' or Judo style throws. There are similarities in Jujutsu/Judo throws to their contemporary western counterparts and medieval combat had its own elaborate system

Again, Talhoffer's fifteenth-century fight book shows the types of throws popular in medieval Europe.

of throws. We only know that the Vikings had an unknown level of expertise in the art of wrestling and of the 'physical' version of the throw.

Saga References

VI

'He crept stealthily to the bed, reached up to the sword, took it down and raised it to strike. Just at the moment when he raised it Grettir sprang up on to the floor, and, seizing the sword with one hand, Grim with the other, hurled him over so that he fell nearly senseless'

Version 1: From a spear thrust a defender grips the spear to disarm, steps to the side and wrenches the weapon from the enemy; for this to be plausible and effective the opponent must be shifted off his centre of balance.

Version 2: During an attack with an axe, an unarmed Viking would have placed his hands on the opponent's grip and on a part of the weapon. From here he then uses natural momentum and leverage to turn the weapon against the opponent.

'Grettir swam beneath the water, keeping close to the bank so that Thorir could not see him, and so reached the bay behind him, where he landed without letting himself be seen. The first Thorir knew of it was when Grettir lifted him up over his head and dashed him down with such violence that the sword fell out of his hand. Grettir got possession of it and without speaking a word cut off his head. So his life ended'

VII

'…and with that he caught hold of him, and lifted him up aloft, and thrust him head down into the broth-kettle. Solvi died at once'

✧ THE DISARM

The 'Disarm' is of course an unarmed Viking taking his opponents' weapon and either sundering it or turning it upon him. The sagas show us two versions of this manoeuvre.

Saga References

People may question an unarmed man placing his unprotected hands on a blade. However, in most cases we must assume that it is the shaft that is grasped. We can point to the archaeological mediaeval finds of people who have been executed post-battle with cuts to the hands, as the condemned men appear to have tried to grab the weapon to save their lives.

V

'Olaf went to the fold-door and struck at him with his spear. Hrapp took the socket of the spear in both hands and wrenched it aside, so that forthwith the spear shaft broke'

VII

'Glum Hilldir's son happened to see what he was about to do, and sprang up at once, and got hold of the axe above Asgrim's hands, and turned the edge at once on Asgrim; for Glum was very strong'

✧ LEAPING THE SPEAR

This is facing a spear attack and either leaping over the spear or pushing its blade into the ground with one's foot.

Saga References

A constant subject that appears in the sagas are games played by Vikings, games that involve the pursuit of manly prowess in such activities that would include: jumping, swimming, ball games, wrestling etc. It is easy to see how these games transferred to war, if we are to believe that they did in fact perform the feat of 'Leaping the Spear'.

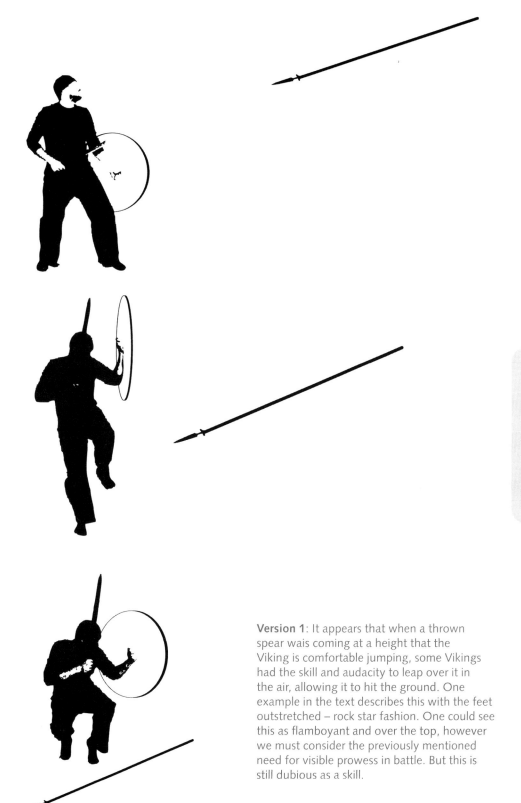

Version 1: It appears that when a thrown spear wais coming at a height that the Viking is comfortable jumping, some Vikings had the skill and audacity to leap over it in the air, allowing it to hit the ground. One example in the text describes this with the feet outstretched – rock star fashion. One could see this as flamboyant and over the top, however we must consider the previously mentioned need for visible prowess in battle. But this is still dubious as a skill.

VII

'Gritgard hurled a spear at Kari, but Kari saw it and sprang up aloft, and the spear missed him'

'Tjorvi turns against Kari and hurls a spear at him. Kari leapt up in the air, and the spear flew below his feet'

'The last ran behind Kari's back, and thrust at him with a spear; Kari caught sight of him, and leapt up as the blow fell, and stretched his legs far apart, and so the blow spent itself on the ground, but Kari jumped down on the spear-shaft, and snapped it in sunder'

'Then Kettle of the Mark rushed at Kari, and thrust at him with his spear. Kari threw up his leg, and the spear stuck in the ground, and Kari leapt on the spear-shaft, and snapped it in sunder'

Version 2: The 'Leg Catch and Snap'; this, although not a leap, has been placed here as a sub-category. It appears that one skill was to 'kick down' a low spear thrust so that the tip went into the earth –as show in the fourth image – this is done with one leg which is then followed with the other that snaps the spear haft in two.

8

HORSE COMBAT

Not many references feature combatants on horseback. The main difference between the Vikings and the people for whom the sagas were written was the greater importance of horse combat in the later period.

✧ THE PRE-COMBAT DISMOUNT

Most men dismount before a combat begins.

Saga References

V

'The men of Salmon-river-Dale now jumped off their horses, and got ready to fight. Hrut bade his men to not trouble themselves about the odds, and to go for them at a rush'

VII

'So those three rode on past them; but the six others then came riding right up to them, and they all leapt off their horses straight away in a body, and turned on Kari and his companion'

✧ THE SPUR GASH

While not a combat move per se the 'Spur Gash' does appear once in the literature. Perhaps it was kind of insult. This event is most likely representative of a later period than the Viking Era. Though spurs have been found in many Viking grave sites.

Saga Reference

VII

'Now, it must be told how Otkell rides faster than he would. He had spurs on his feet, and so he gallops down over the ploughed field, and neither of them sees the other; and just as Gunnar stands upright, Otkell rides down upon him and drives one of the spurs into Gunnar's ear, and gives him a great gash, and it bleeds at once much'

He gashes the opponent's face with a spur or bludgeons thim with the stirrup while on horseback.

9

COMBINATION MOVES

The following chapter looks at a series of combination moves in detail. They are designed to be as realistic and historically representative as possible.

✧ COMBINATION 1

This is an entrapment manoeuvre by two aggressors that leaves the Viking Vali dead. Vali attacks Bersi, which allows Halldor to flank him and strike a cutting blow. This makes Vali turn on his rear attacker whereupon Bersi uses the technique of 'Striking the centre of the back' and kills Vali. The age of Halldor tells us so much about Viking culture and society: 'Halldor was twelve winters old when these doings came to pass.'

Saga Reference

/

'But when he was on the way back again, out came Bersi and Halldor to meet him. Bersi had a halberd in one hand and a staff in the other, and Halldor had Whitting. As soon as Vali saw them he turned and hewed at Bersi. Halldor came at his back and fleshed

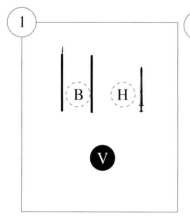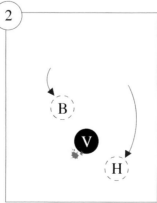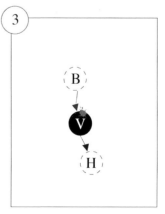

Here we see Bersi (B) and Halldor (H) close in on Vali (V), flank and kill him. Bersi is holding a halberd and a staff while Halldor has a sword.

Whitting in his hough-sinews. Thereupon he turned sharply and fell upon Halldor. Then Bersi set the halberd-point betwixt his shoulders. That was his death-wound'

✧ COMBINATION 2

This displays a 'Low-Level Leg Strike' by an aggressor who is then disembowelled by his enemy, who uses a sword thrust to his stomach. This combination is a perfect example of a warrior continuing his attack even though he has been incapacitated or has received a death wound. The martial artist must always guard his or her exit from an attack – and in deadly combat both people can die and possibly often did.

This encounter holds a great lesson for medieval combat: always guard yourself when you feel you have delivered a fatal blow, as it will take a short while for the blow to register and take effect, in which time the opponent may react and as in this case, 'win' the combat. In this case, the severing of a leg will end the fight but the swordsman on the left celebrated this victory too early, which gave the soon to be dying man a window of opportunity in the short time he has before he succumbs to the loss of blood.

Saga Reference

II

> 'But one stroke Thorod fetched at Thorbiorn, and smote off his foot at the ankle-joint; but nonetheless he fought on, and thrust forth his sword into Thorod's belly, so that he fell, and his gut burst out'

✧ COMBINATION 3

This displays a thrust by the aggressor Thorir who over-extends his pole-arm thrust, which is used against him by the defender. Uspak the defender uses the parry and cut to allow the aggressor to overextend and fall to his knees and in a position where he is open to attack.

Saga Reference

IV

> 'Thorir had a bear-bill in his hand, and therewith he ran at Uspak and smote at him, but Uspak put the thrust from him, and whereas Thorir had thrown all his might into the blow, and there was nought before the bill, he fell on his knees and fell forward. Then Uspak smote Thorir on the back with: his axe, and loud rang the stroke'

✧ COMBINATION 4

This displays two men attacking a defender who is on higher ground. The attackers thrust at the defender who has to bend backwards to execute his parry. The aggressors then take advantage of this and use 'Low-Level Strike to the Legs' to disable him. Perhaps the Vikings fought as combat-pairs as a matter of course, one using the openings that the other created to kill the enemy.

Combination 4. As can be seen, the warrior on the left makes to thrust at the man defending on the wall. In a pre-arranged attack, the man on the right takes advantage of the gap his companion has created and strikes at the defender's legs.

THE ILLUSTRATED GUIDE TO VIKING MARTIAL ARTS

'Onund was stepping out with one foot on to the bulwark, and as he was striking they made a thrust at him with a spear; in parrying it he bent backwards, and at that moment a man on the forecastle of the king's ship struck him and took off his leg below the knee, disabling him at a blow'

✧ COMBINATION 5

A projectile results in the dropping of a principal weapon. The opponent then takes up Atli's own sword and uses a 'Low-Level Strike to the Legs' to disable and then delivers a death blow.

In this situation, the defender has thrown a stone at the opponent as an improvised weapon, so that he can take advantage of the gap or window it creates, in this case the use of a fallen sword.

'just then Atli got a blow on his hand from a stone, and down fell his sword. Hrut caught up the sword, and cut his foot from under him. After that he dealt him his death-blow'

✧ COMBINATION 6

Thiostolf attacks Hrut with an axe. Hrut then makes an 'Evasion' move and simultaneously uses a 'Disarm' strike with his left hand to Thiostolf's axe hand. The second step Hrut takes is to execute a 'Low-level Strike to the Legs' to cut off Thiosof's leg and it appears he barges him to push the now one-legged man over. To finish, Hrut makes an 'Overhead Cut' and kills his opponent. This is a fantastic example of the fluidity and speed of such combat. The 'Disarm' is interesting as Hrut use his empty hand. In Japanese martial arts this skill is akin to *Koppo-jutsu*, which is a 'bone-breaking' skill and consists of striking joints, sometimes used to open the hand when defending against knife or weapon attacks.

Saga Reference

VII

'Thiostolf cuts at Hrut. Hrut got out of the way of the stroke by a quick turn, and at the same time struck the back of the axe so smartly with a side-long blow of his left hand, that it flew out of Thiostolf's grasp. Then Hrut made a blow with his sword in his right hand at Thiostolf's leg, just above the knee, and cut it almost off so that it hung by a little piece, and sprang in upon him at the same time, and thrust him hard back. After that he smote him on the head, and dealt him his death-blow'

A strike to the back of the hand to disarm the opponent. This must not be an exaggerated movement but an up-close, short, very powerful – and unexpected – strike. If done correctly it should make the weapon 'fly' out of the opponent's hand and leave him disarmed.

✧ COMBINATION 7

This displays an attacker running up from behind and probably trying to use the 'Strike to the Centre of the Back' at which his opponent turns around and parries, which he then combines with a 'Disarm' using the prongs of his own weapon.

Using prongs, hilts and any protrusion is something often missed in our appreciation of medieval fighting. Here, the defender must parry the blow and turn that parry into a fluid hook motion and then use the natural weight of the body to disarm the opponent by catching his weapon on any cross-bar or hook.

Saga Reference

VII

'Skamkell ran behind Gunnar's back and makes a blow at him with a great axe. Gunnar turned short round upon him and parries the blow with the bill, and caught the axe under one of its horns with such a wrench that it flew out of Skamkell's hand away into the river'

✧ COMBINATION 8

This displays an aggressor using a 'Low-level Strike to the Legs' where the opponent jumps above the cut and then strikes with a spear, either in mid-flight or just as he lands. The jump must have been only knee height and would be considered a small 'hop' over a strike to the lower leg.

Saga Reference

VII

'Otkell smites at Gunnar with his sword, and aims at his leg just below the knee, but Gunnar leapt up into the air, so he misses him. Then Gunnar thrusts at him the bill and the blow goes through him'

Combination 8. In this version, the defender has leapt over the sword stroke to his legs and landed, then waited for the attacker to move to his next strike and as the attacker has moved to take his next blow the defender has found a gap and used his spear to thrust him through.

✧ COMBINATION 9

This displays an aggressor running upon the warrior Skarphedinn and thrusting at him. We then see Skarphedinn 'sunder' the spear with an axe. He then makes a powerful second blow that is either an 'Overhead Cut' or a 'Shield Cleave', which forces the shield back and allows Skarphedinn to kill the aggressor with a blow to the head. This combination demonstrates how the movement between strikes, cuts and thrusts would have been extremely fluid and fast paced.

The spearman has thrust forward but the defender on the right has blocked the spear and cut through the shaft, or at least restricted its movement, from here and depending on which windows of opportunity open up, the axe-man can make his counter strike.

Saga Reference

VII

'Then Hroald Auzur's son ran up to where Skarphedinn stood, and thrust at him. Skarphedinn hewed the spearhead off the shaft as he held it, and made another stroke at him, and the axe fell on the top of the shield, and dashed back the whole shield on Hroald's body, but the upper horn of the axe caught him on the brow, and he fell at full length on his back, and was dead at once'

✧ COMBINATION 10

This displays a very rare and interesting insight to 'Combat Teams' or Viking tactics on a small scale. On one side we have an archer protected by shield-bearers and the said archer is a magnificent shot. Thus, the defenders concoct a plan to shoot within a fraction

The 'sharp shooting' archer protected by two shield-bearers. The enemy concocted a plan to have arrows shot to the outside of the defenders' space, making them move the shields to protect against the arrows coming in from the periphery, this opened up a gap for another archer to kill the 'sniper'.

of a second of each other, the first to shift the protecting shield and the second to use the opening created to kill the archer. There can be no doubt about the existence of such skilful archers; through documented experimentation in recent years we have seen the levels that some people can achieve with a replica bow. It is logical to have had 'sharp shooters' of the day in the field of archery.

Saga Reference

XVIII

'While the Vindlanders were storming the castle, their king and his chiefs were out of the battle. At one place there was a man among the Vindlanders shooting with a bow, and killing a man for every arrow; and two men stood before him, and covered him with their shields. Then Saemund Husfreyja said to his son Asmund, that they should both shoot together at this bowman. 'But I will shoot at the man who holds the shield before him.' He did so, and he knocked the shield down a little before the man; and in the same instant Asmund shot between the shields, and the arrow hit the bowman in the forehead, so that it came out at his neck, and he fell down dead'

GROUP COMBAT

Group combat is a norm and gang fights, 'pack style hunting', are all part of the Viking fighting system. Real fighting often consists of battling with more than one person at a time and it is clear from historical records across the warrior cultures of the world that one man can kill many, with skill, weapons and determination. But if he must face multiple assailants then at some stage the battle becomes unwinnable.

✧ GROUP COMBAT 1

Group Combat 1 displays a group of assailants thrusting at Arnkel the defender, against which he uses the technique of 'Sundering Weapons' to smash the spear shafts. Then two of the assailants come upon him with swords drawn, to which he again makes an unknown strike at them. By this time the defender has reached his weapons and shield and defends himself. However, it appears that the troops lay about him and give him wounds until he weakens and dies.

Saga Reference
IV

'Now when Snorri and his folk came to the garth, it is not told that any words befell there, but straightway they set on Arnkel, and chiefly with spear-thrust, which Arnkel

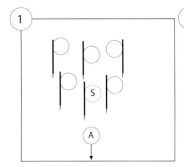
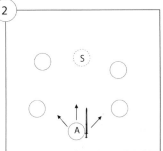
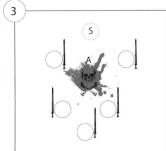

The group attack the defender, who using an improvised weapon breaks their spears. However, to no avail, as they surround and wound him until he can defend himself, no more.

put from him with the sledge-runner, and many of the spear-shafts were broken thereby, nor was Arnkel wounded; but when they had spent their shot-weapons, then Thorleif Kimbi ran at the garth and leapt up on to it with sword drawn, and Arnkel smote at him with the sledge-runner, and Thorleif dropped down away from the stroke out of the garth, and the runner smote against the garth wall, and up therefrom flew a piece of frozen turf; but the sledge-runner was broken, and fell apart part. Arnkel had laid his sword and shield against a hayrick, and now he took up his weapons and defended himself therewith; but now he began to gather wounds, and withal they came up into the garth about him. Then Arnkel leapt up on to the hayrick, and defended himself thence for a space, but such was the end of the matter that he fell, and they covered him over there in the garth with hay; and thereafter Snorri and his folk returned home to Holyfell'

✧ GROUP COMBAT 2

This displays a complex but fast paced fight involving four men. Thord uses a spear thrust at Thorleif. Thorleif protects himself with his shield, which results in the attacker Thord slipping on the rocks and falling. Thorleif seeing his chance, jumps on top of his fallen attacker with what is probably an overhead cut. When he makes this attack we see another man, Freystein, jump with Thorleif to aid him in the kill. The fourth man is Steinthor, and he is on the side of the fallen Thord. Steinthor comes in to protect the fallen Thord with his shield. At the same time that he covers his friend Steinthor uses a 'Low-level Strike to the Legs' and cuts the leg off Thorleif, the man attacking his fallen comrade. Upon seeing his ally injured, Freystein thrusts at Steinthor. However, the skilled Steinthor sees the blow coming and 'Leaps the Spear' and then cuts his attacker down with a 'Strike to the Neck'. The reference to 'shoe-spikes' may be anachronistic. The usual Viking footwear was little more than a leather ankle slipper. See later section on the spiked shoe in chapter 11. (Interestingly, long laces may have been a sign of status.)

Group Combat 3: The strike with the pole-arm to the sword of the right-hand man must be strong enough to temporarily disarm him, at which point the defender takes the head of the man on the left. The defender must follow up here and finish or contend with the man on the right.

'Now slow work was the winning of the skerry, but when they had been thereat a long while, Thord Wall-eye made a dash at it, and would thrust at Thorleif Kimbi with a spear, for he was ever the foremost of his men. The thrust smote the shield of Thorleif, but even as Thord Wall-eye laboured over the blow his feet failed him on the slippery floe, and he fell on his back and slipped headforemost down from the skerry. Thorleif Kimbi leapt after him to smite him dead before he could get to his feet again, and Freystein Rascal followed Thorleif, and he had shoe-spikes on his feet. Then Steinthor ran thereto, and cast his shield over Thord even as Thorleif fetched a blow at him, and with the other hand he smote at Thorleif Kimbi, and smote the leg from him below the knee; and while that was a-doing Freystein Rascal thrust at Steinthor, aiming at his middle; and when Steinthor saw that, he leapt up aloft, and the thrust went between his legs, and these three things, whereof we have told even now, he did in one and the same nick of time. Then he ran to Freystein, and smote him on the neck with his sword, and loud was the clatter of that stroke. So he cried withal: 'Art smitten, Rascal?'

✧ GROUP COMBAT 3

This displays a parry that leads to a Disarm as Gunnar defends himself. Gunnar uses his sword, which is in his other hand, to decapitate Thorkel with a strike to the neck. Gunnar is using both a pole-arm and a sword and disarms the first attack with a parry and then decapitates another man with his second hand.

Saga Reference

VII

'Bork made a blow at Gunnar, and Gunnar threw his bill so hard in the way, that the sword flew out of Bork's hand; then he sees Thorkel standing on his other hand within stroke of sword. The defending Gunnar was standing with his body swayed a little on one side and makes a sweep with his sword, he catches Thorkel on the neck, and off flew his head'

MISCELLANEOUS ASPECTS OF COMBAT

This chapter considers the sections of the sagas that could not be categorised above and that stand outside the normal realm of combat techniques.

✧ THE WAY OF DEATH

The 'Way of Death' is the concept of the 'soul' being tempered by a warrior culture, forging a disciplined warrior who has no fear of death. We see the concept of life without fear of death in most warrior cultures, where honour takes pride of place or where to die in battle is the greatest achievement there can be in life. In the sagas we have seen Vikings turn and flee, we have seen them attack from behind and we have seen them attack like a pack of wolves. But once in a while we see the warrior archetype, the one who is the bravest of men and the most skilled amongst his peers. One could attribute this to poetic licence used to thrill an audience, which may be true some of the time. As a society we need hero figures to worship and we need an ideal to pursue. That being said, the reality of bravery is not lost in the mists of time. We know of heroic deeds in both of the World Wars; we have read historically accurate stories of men giving up their lives, heroes. We also know of the fanaticism of the Japanese in the Second World War who gave their lives in great numbers to uphold their own concept of honour. It is surely not hard to conceive that the nearly perfect warrior can exist from time to time within warrior cultures.

Saga References

II

'Thorgisl the Hewer spared nought; he deemed great scathe wrought him by the death of his son. He was the mightiest man of his hands, and better with weapons than other men. He heweth on either hand and deemeth life no better than death'

III

'Now was that battle fierce and fell, and though Sigmund were old, yet most hardily he fought, and was ever the foremost of his men; no shield or byrny might hold against him, and he went ever through the ranks of his foemen on that day, and no man might see

Here the swordsman is committing suicide by placing the sword to his armpit and pushing the blade through his heart – in the Saga this is done by a female.

In this case, the swordsman is 'falling' on his sword by placing it against his chest and allowing the blade to strike deeply into the heart.

how things would fare between them; many an arrow and many a spear was aloft in air that day, and so his spae-wrights wrought for him that he got no wound, and none can tell over the tale of those who fell before him, and both his arms were red with blood, even to the shoulders'

'Well could he wield sword, and cast forth spear, shoot shaft, and hold shield, bend bow, back horse, and do all the goodly deeds that he learned in his youth's days'

V

'…but the men of Salmon-river-Dale very soon found that in Hrut they had to deal with one for whom they were no match, for now he slew two men at every onslaught'

VII

'He was a tall man in growth, and a strong man, best skilled in arms of all men. He could cut or thrust or shoot if he chose as well with his left as with his right hand, and he smote so swiftly with his sword, that three seemed to flash through the air at once. He was the best shot with the bow of all men, and never missed his mark. He could leap more than his own height, with all his war-gear, and as far backwards as forwards. He could swim like a seal, and there was no game in which it was any good for any one to strive with him; and so it has been said that no man was his match'

✧ THE WAY OF SUICIDE

Modern western society with its Christian elements still shaping our secular age see suicide as negative. But each culture of course has a different understanding of the 'rules' of the after life and the dignity that accompanies suicide. The Vikings were men and women born in a relatively violent age and tempered by their society, however they were humans like you and me and they share certain traits. One has to remember that in a world of religious beliefs and to a people who have firm values, some actions that are inexplicable to us, are in fact normal to others. Sometimes of course humans do unexplained things, and logic is not a factor.

Saga References

The second quotation describes a 'classic' Roman suicide. Hake falls upon his sword.

III

'Now she bade bring forth much gold, and bade all those come thither who would have wealth: then she caught up a sword, and thrust it under her armpit, and sank aside upon the pillows, and said, "Come, take gold whoso will!"'

IX

'Hake got up and went after them a while; but when he came to the ice on the lake, he turned his sword-hilt to the ground and let himself fall upon the point, so that the sword went through him. He was buried under a mound on the banks of the lake'

✧ CLAIMING THE HEAD

This is the process of taking the decapitated head of an enemy for display or as a warning. We must not use the term head-hunting as there is no evidence that the Vikings killed simply to claim the head. The Vikings' attitude is similar to that of the Japanese. The medieval Japanese took heads as proof of victory and to collect reward, as in the Viking sagas. One can only speculate what they did with the heads afterwards, however, as the third quotation suggests, they may have kept them.

For comparison, in Japanese feudal society the head was taken and made ready to be presented to a lord. There were intricate points of etiquette that dictated the way the head should be presented, systematised according to social standing and consideration of the enemy's ghost. It was cleaned and prepared and presented to the lord on a 'plate' or 'board'. The lord was protected from the head by an archer, and he could only glance at the head from behind a fan; a war cry was given and then the head was taken away. On certain occasions the lord had to make the ritualistic cutting of a *Kuji-kiri* grid in the air before the head, for protection. The first two references indicate a similarly ritualistic approach in the placing of the decapitated head between the thighs.

The body lying down with the head between the legs.

Saga References

VI

'When the thrall had spoken, the faintness which had come over Grettir left him. He drew his short sword, cut off Glam's head and laid it between his thighs'

Grettir then drew his sword Jokulsnaut, cut off the head of the howedweller and laid it between his thighs.

VII

'After that they slew Kol, and Thrain cut off his head, and they threw the trunk overboard, but kept his head'

XIX

'Sigurd asked which of his lads had most desire to go in against Beintein, which he called brave man's work; but none was very hurried to make ready for it. While they were discussing this matter Sigurd rushed into the house, past Beintein. Beintein struck at him, but missed. Sigurd turned instantly on Beintein; and after exchanging blows, Sigurd gave him his death-stroke, and came out presently bearing his head in his hands'

Here the body is sat up with the head between the legs.

A warrior keeps his prize head.

✧ ARMED AND READY?

Films often portray medieval warriors in armour and helmets most of the time. They sit down to meals in full plate armour and go about their daily lives geared for war. When did the Viking actually wear his sword, when would he have his mail or leather protection on, where did he keep his helmet? Armour is kept in a box or on a stand when not in use in most medieval societies. As a samurai kept his sword with him, did the Vikings? There are references to this and yes, we can see the Vikings kept their swords handy, and the second quotation shows us that some slept armed and ready when they were on watch. But when not on alert the Viking warriors would be dressed in woollen cloaks, woollen or linen shirts and breeches. *Lin-klædi*, linen clothing, is often mentioned in the Icelandic sagas. In graves, the sword or fighting knife is not worn by the body but is put alongside it; and in the sagas when a warrior puts on his sword it is remarked upon. Both these points suggest that the sword perhaps was not, in fact, worn as a matter of course.

169

Saga References

VI

'He drew his sword Jokulsnaut and tied a loop round the handle which he passed over his wrist, because he thought that he could carry out his plans better if his hand were free'

XX

'They changed the watch with each other in the night, and those who had been before on watch lay down and slept; but all completely armed. It was their custom, when they went to sleep, that each should have his helmet on his head, his shield over him, sword under the head, and the right hand on the sword-handle'

The sleeping Viking ready for war.

✧ THE SPIKED SHOES

'Spiked Shoes', if they were indeed worn, would allow the wearer better grip on the ice or in rough terrain. People in the martial arts community will immediately bring to mind the Japanese foot spike and look for similarities. However, there is no record of the Japanese foot spikes being used as an offensive weapon. Though a trained warrior could have made use of them if the occasion arose.

Saga References

The 'snow-shoes' of the third quotation are the same as modern snow shoes.

IV

'Freystein Rascal followed Thorleif, and he had shoe-spikes on his feet'

'…but Freystein stood firm on his spiked shoes'

XIV

'He was better than any man at running on snow-shoes'

The Viking in the snow using 'spiked shoes'

EFFECTIVENESS OF WEAPONS

Anyone can see the true destructive power of the Viking weaponry by simply studying the many videos of people 'cut testing' Viking swords on the internet. The wounds described in the sagas are readiily inflicted and can be accepted as truth. The only doubts that arise are to do with those blows that are said to shatter helms. We know that it is possible to do minor damage to mail, as it described in the sagas, we also know that cutting through a shield is certainly possible; but people dispute the ability to cut a helm. This has not been proven or disproven, but one must remember that not all helmets were metal, some were of leather and bone.

Inferior products were on the market. Inferior swords that did not make the grade may have found their way into the hands of the warriors. We can find examples of this in the quotations below, of swords too brittle or too malleable. We should think of the weapons of the Vikings not as a horde of gleaming treasures but of a varied collection of tools, from the humble wood axe, to the second-hand, shoddy blade, all the way up to an outstanding heirloom, the creation of a master craftsman. The arrestingly beautiful image in the second quotation should not blind us to the fact that this perfectly honed edge has been created to destroy.

Saga References

III

'"Behold thy smithying, Regin!" and therewith smote it into the anvil, and the sword brake; so he cast down the brand, and bade him forge a better'

'Then he praised the sword much, and thereafter went to the river with a lock of wool, and threw the wool upstream, and it fell asunder when it met the sword. Then was Sigurd glad, and went home'

IV

'But in the home-field at Mewlithe men found a hand whereas they had fought, and it was shown to Thorarin; he saw that it was a woman's hand, and asked where Aud was; it was told him that she lay in bed. Then he went to her, and asked whether she were wounded; she bade him pay no heed to that, but he was ware withal that her hand had been hewn off. Then he called to his mother, and bade her bind up the wound'

'Then were Thorbrand's sons brought home to Holyfell and their wounds bound up. Thorod Thorbrandson had so great a wound in the back of his neck that he might not hold his head straight'

'Then Snorri the Priest drew his hand down his throat, and found an arrow sticking athwart his gullet and the roots of the tongue. Then Snorri the Priest took drawing-tongs and pulled out the arrow, and then Snorri Thorbrandson fell to his meat'

'So then befell a great battle, and Steinthor was at the head of his own folk, and smote on either hand of him; but the fair-wrought sword bit not, and when as it smote armour, oft he must straighten it under his foot'

VI

'There was no resistance in him for he was already dead from his wounded leg; his thigh was all mortified up to the rectum. Many more wounds they gave him, but little or no blood flowed.'

'They said this was unnecessary, as the man was dead before. 'I will do more,' he said, and struck two or three blows at Grettir's neck before he took off his head.'

'Now they all rose up and ran at them, and Modolf Kettle's son was quickest of them, and thrust at Kari with his spear. Kari had his shield before him, and the blow fell on it, and the spear stuck fast in the shield. Then Kari twists the shield so smartly, that the spear snapped short off, and then he drew his sword and smote at Modolf; but Modolf made a cut at him too, and Kari's sword fell on Modolf's hilt, and glanced off it on to Modolf's wrist, and took the arm off, and down it fell, and the sword too. Then Kari's sword passed on into Modolf's side, and between his ribs, and so Modolf fell down and was dead on the spot.'

'Grani had his shield before him, and the spear came on the shield and passed right through it, and into Grani's thigh just below the small guts, and through the limb, and so on, pinning him to the ground, and he could not get rid of the spear before his fellows drew him off it, and carried him away on their shields, and laid him down in a dell.'

IX

'...and there was great battle, in which King Halfdan was victorious; and just as King Sigtryg and his troops were turning about to fly, an arrow struck him under the left arm, and he fell dead.'

CONCLUSION

The Viking martial arts consisted of a set of 'techniques' that were common to the people across Scandinavia and they were represented in the sagas. Remembering that some of the sagas are hundreds years apart in writing, we can see that a definite series of moves is found throughout, moves that are no doubt shared by many martial styles across the ancient and medieval world. The Viking system shares many techniques with later European medieval martial texts and elements of the writings of *fechtmeister* Hans Talhoffer in southern Germany, for example, can be found in the Viking arts.

Whilst recognising that getting to the realities of Viking combat is made difficult by the changes made in the sagas to suit a later 'knightly' audience, we have here a glimpse of a form of combat that was continuous between 800 and 1400.

Even if the combat in all of the sagas across all the time periods was a direct reflection of the experience of the audience they entertained and had little connection to the Vikings, and if all the techniques shown in this book are in fact early second millennium forms of combat, we have still created something of a first. The earliest illustrated document in existence for western medieval combat is the MS I.33 manuscript held by Leeds Armouries and dates to 1290. So the moves described in the sagas are as important as this now famous manuscript in the search for early western combat arts. I of course do not think that the techniques demonstrated here are from a later date – I believe the sagas tell the truth about the Vikings, or enough of the truth to say that this is how the fearsome warriors of the north fought.

Above: The Viking raid on Lindisfarne, 793. 'Never before has such terror appeared in Britain as we have now suffered from a pagan race,' wrote the scholar Alcuin.

Below: The Battle of Stamford Bridge, 1066. Legend has it during the eventual rout of the Vikings by Harold Godwinson's Saxon army, at one stage a huge Viking blocked the bridge and slew 40 men with an axe. Both images courtesy of renowned artist Victor Ambrus, from his beautiful *Battlefield Panoramas – From the Siege of Troy to D-Day*.